Raisins and Almonds

Rachel Rosemarin

Raisins and Almonds

Practical Advice for Sensitive Parenting

FELDHEIM PUBLISHERS
JERUSALEM NEW YORK

Male and female are used interchangeably throughout this book when referring to children. In most instances, the examples can be applied to both boys and girls.

First published in Hebrew as *Tzimukim u'Shkeidim* and distributed by Feldheim Publishers (2006)

Translated into English by Sandy Bloom
Illustrations by Ruth Beifus

Also by the author: *Mama Used to Say* (Jerusalem: Feldheim Publishers, 2000)

ISBN 978-1-58330-951-3

FELDHEIM PUBLISHERS
POB 43163/ Jerusalem, Israel

208 Airport Executive Park
Nanuet, NY 10954

www.feldheim.com

10 9 8 7 6 5 4 3 2 1

Printed in Israel

Library of Congress Cataloging-in-Publication Data
Rozmarin, Rahel.
[Tsimukim u-shekedim. English]
Raisins and almonds : practical advice for sensitive parenting / by Rachel Rosemarin ; translated into English by Sandy Bloom.
p. cm.
ISBN-13: 978-1-58330-951-3
1. Jewish religious education of children. 2. Child rearing--Religious aspects--Judaism. 3. Parenting--Religious aspects--Judaism. 4. Parent and child (Jewish law) I. Title.
BM103.R67513 2007
296.7'4--dc22

2007023463

Contents

Dedicated with great esteem
to Mothers in Israel
who labor unstintingly
in raising their children
and aspire to creating
nachas ruach for Hashem.

Acknowledgments

First and foremost, I offer my heartfelt praise to Hashem; *shir v'shevach* to the Blessed Creator, Who has brought me to where I am today.

My thanks and blessings to my dear friend, Mrs. Chaya Kiel, who is blessed with talent and understanding and who accompanied the writing of this book from its very inception. She advised me, edited my work with an artist's hand, and also contributed her wisdom and refined taste to improve the "fragrance" of the book.

Special thanks to Mrs. Ruth Beifus. Her illustrations in this book reflect both her artistic talents and her warm emotions. You did a beautiful job, Ruth.

My thanks also go to Mrs. Amira Chachamovitz. She was of great help during the earliest stages of the book, watering the first literary buds with the wisdom they needed to grow and flower.

Thank you to the editorial, design, and production staff at Feldheim Publishers, Jerusalem. The beauty and content of this book reflect your professional touch.

Our praise and gratitude again go to Hashem Yisbarach for the great *nachas* my husband and I derive from our children and grandchildren, *ken yirbu*. Observing you, my dear ones, has enriched my life, taught me understanding, and given me wisdom.

And last but not least, cheers to you, my dear daughter-in-law and daughters, for your loving devotion and dedication to the success of my book.

As always, I pray for and aspire to continual *siyatta diShmaya*.

Rachel Rosemarin (neé Sankevitz)

Preface

A Few Words

HERE WE ARE AGAIN this week, my dear friends, mothers in our parenting group. Again we sit in a circle, each of you with your individual needs and issues but all of us united around one objective—how to improve the family atmosphere. Many times you have asked, "What can I do?" or "Tell me how to solve this problem," as we analyzed situations that arise in family life and dealt with *chinuch* (childrearing) issues. One idea led to the next, one suggestion built upon another, as we slowly amassed the "Raisins and Almonds" of childrearing —sweet and tasty principles and concepts. Thus this book was born.

Our book is different from other parenting books. It does not profess to be a methodical reference book on *chinuch*, nor is it a collection of comprehensive articles on the subject. Instead, it contains an assortment of thought-provoking ideas for discussion together with a collection of practical tips (the "Tasty Morsels" section at the end of each chapter) that serve as "condiments" to enhance the family atmosphere.

When I finished committing everything to writing, I debated what name to give the book. I looked for a name that would reflect my desire to give you, my dear mothers, fine and useful tools and tips for your important life mission of *chinuch banim*. Then it occurred to me to use the old but beautiful expression, "Raisins and Almonds," as a metaphor for something of high quality, something good and useful, something that one wants to lovingly bestow on her friend. And that was my intention in writing this book. "Raisins and Almonds," or "Rozhinkes mit Mandlen," is the name of an old, popular Yiddish lullaby in which a Jewish mother rocks her baby boy to sleep and sings that her son will grow up to become a *talmid chacham* and write *sifrei kodesh*.

Yehi ratzon, my dear mothers, that you will enjoy reading this book and derive much benefit from it in building homes full of true Jewish *simchah*, homes of Torah, for all eternity.

Raisins and Almonds

1 My Mother, My Teacher

CHAZAL DEFINE THE ROLE of father and mother with the terms, "*avi mori*" (literally, "my father, my teacher") and "*imi morasi*" (literally, "my mother, my teacher").

What is the difference between being a parent and being a teacher? Parents are supposed to support their children from the moment of their birth, at all times and in every situation. This support and sustenance is achieved through love, encouragement, emotional involvement, attentiveness, and acceptance. Teachers, on the other hand, are supposed to guide, lead and navigate; delegate authority; give the child space to "do his own thing" and set limits. Chazal viewed the essence of parenthood as the integration of these two roles—providing both support and guidance for the proper growth and *chinuch* of the child. We will expand on the essence of this integration below.

Avi-Imi; My Father, My Mother

Chazal distinguishes the motherly role from the teaching role in that the former precedes the latter, as in *imi morasi—ima*, mother, precedes *morah,* teacher. Indeed, the infant needs a supportive mother from the moment of birth and throughout the years, "like a suckling upon its mother" (*Tehillim* 131:2). The mother's support and sustenance is also the basis for her child's spiritual development, and draws out his latent strengths until he can realize his potential on his own.

Limitless encouragement and support that only a mother can impart is what helps a child create a positive self-image. We can liken the inner world of a human being to a picture album containing innumerable snapshots. The pictures represent experiences from the moment of birth and their imprint on the soul. It is clear that the content of these pictures have implications for the child's self-image and coping abilities. Thus the album will have maximal positive impact if positive, smiling photos make up the majority of the pictures, together with encouraging tapes that resonate with agreeable compliments. Then, when life visits your child with inevitable harsh moments, he can find support in the comforting words preserved in his memory.

What moments would we want to preserve in this album? Let us take the example of a child who succeeds for a moment in restraining himself and overcoming his negative impulses—to hit his baby brother, for example. If this instance of self-control is not lost in the ocean of daily experiences, if his parents are wise enough to preserve the moment by emphasizing to the child the merits of his accomplishment and the *nachas* they enjoyed from his behavior—then this moment will remain indelibly etched in the album. The child will then be able to access these positive memories in his album to cope with future trials and tribulations. Appropriate parental feedback to a child's success experiences gives him the courage to try, and succeed, again.

Support includes giving, and what is greater than a mother's selfless giving to her child? There is no need to wax at length about this as it is self-understood, but there is another, less familiar type of giving that mothers should adopt due to its educational value: giving at the initiative of the mother, before the child even asks. This kind of giving instills in the child the perception that his mother thinks about him and tries to fulfill his needs in every sphere, even before he notices that he is lacking something and calls her attention to it. This feeling bestows calmness and security on the child that allow him to grow and develop without worrying constantly about his basic needs. Thus when parents give at their own initiative, the child feels that he has received a valuable gift. But when the parent only gives when the child demands it, the child feels like a taker (or a grabber). In this case the act of giving does not give him a sense of satisfaction, but instead creates the drive to demand more and more, to take advantage so as not to lose out. A parent who initiates giving, as opposed to the parent who is dragged into it, fills her child with confidence and serenity.

Motherly support is also imparted through verbally expressing trust in a child. This strengthens the child's belief in herself and her own abilities. It is important to give a child challenges that she is capable of overcoming, and to praise her after achieving the goal. It is even important to praise a child for things she carries out imperfectly, as this encourages her to try again next time. In addition, it is advisable to consult with the child on issues about which she has an opinion, and then to respect her opinion.

Words of personal appreciation are invaluable, such as when you make your child aware of how her actions helped you and made you happy. These include statements such as, "You really lightened my load when you watched your brother" or "Thanks to your help in putting the vegetables away in the refrigerator, I was able to put the baby to sleep."

Try to phrase your appreciation using sentences that contain three elements: "I saw…I felt…That's what I call…." For example: "I **saw** how you picked up the peels from the floor. I **felt happy** to see you do that. That's what I call **responsibility**!" Repeated statements such as these help the child recognize his positive character traits. This knowledge will remain with him during periods of temptation and give him the strength to pick himself up after he falls. Words of trust and encouragement found in one's "memory box" are a powerful motivation to activity and growth. The positive words that have accumulated within the child's psyche will enable him not to drown in failures and disappointments, but will instead anchor him firmly in his place, with *siyatta diShmaya*.

My Father-Teacher, My Mother-Teacher

As mentioned above, parenthood also includes teaching, as the parent fulfills the role of leader and guide. *Morasi* means one who leads and is not led. Parents must convey polite but firm authority. Their presence should be felt—they hold a very clear place in the family hierarchy. A parent is not a friend; he may act in a friendly manner but his children need him as a parent, not as a peer or a pal.

A parent must guide. Sometimes we forget this and expect our children to understand things on their own, since we know that children do learn a great deal even without direction. However, we must remember that the lion's share of *chinuch* is not acquired automatically and parents must help the child to mold his behavior.

How should you guide? Here are some suggestions.

Every encounter with a new reality necessitates guidance. Preliminary instruction can go a long way in averting sticky, unpleasant situations, ambiguity, and disagreement, as well as in preventing arguments and faultfinding on both sides. A preliminary "briefing" before a new experience can clarify the behavior we expect from our children. Sometimes we explain the reasons for our demands, sometimes we allow our children to express their opinions and request modifications in the rules, and often we also remind them of the unpleasant consequences of violating our instructions.

Let us take the example of a family on their way to a shopping trip. The mother can explain to the children where they are going, what is the objective of the trip, and what behaviors are expected of them both on the way and once they arrive. She can tell them how much money she is prepared to spend and what she is not prepared to buy.

This will go a long way toward forestalling arguments such as who will sit near the window or whether Ima is buying pizza for supper, and it will be clear that no one buys clothing above the price that Ima has decided in advance.

V'shinantam l'vanecha—You shall repeat them to your children. We must remind ourselves over and over that children don't learn from one experience. Even though we've said something once, we may have to repeat it again and again until the instruction is internalized. Slowly but surely it will become a habit, and then we can continue inculcating additional habits.

Try to *adjust the instruction to the age and level of the specific child* and then *transmit the message clearly and in the appropriate order*: "The peel goes in the garbage and the fruit goes in the bowl," "We give a coin for tzedakah with our right hand," "We make our beds in the morning," and so on.

Educational guidance may also necessitate *a number of short, clear sentences* such as, "In our house, we expect each person to place the dish he used in the sink," or "Let's make the *berachah* out loud and be *zocheh* to answer Amen." These kinds of statements strengthen the cohesiveness of family members, who share a sense of belonging and follow the same rules.

When we instruct our children we should also *take into account the possibility of failure or mishap*, and be ready to *accept both with understanding and good will*: “No man truly understands a *davar halachah* without misunderstanding it previously”; “One can always repair his mistake.”

Parents must act authoritatively in order to fulfill their roles as leaders and teachers. “I am in charge here, and I use my authority to guide you in the correct path”—this is the message that all parents must broadcast in their childrearing efforts. This clarifies to the child the role of the parent in the family versus her place as the child, and teaches her to delay gratification and control her behavior before her parent’s position of authority.

Some of the main characteristics of authoritative guidance include: **seriousness** that will cause the child to obey, combined with **politeness** devoid of anger or displays of power that invite confrontation, and **brevity**: “Please stop jumping”; “Please put on your pajamas and get into bed.”

Often, words are not enough for young children. Instead, try to *match words to accompanying actions*, such as leading a child to his room while repeating, "It's time to go to sleep."

When we address young children, we must be extra careful to *speak clearly and not vaguely*. We should not speak complicated, complex sentences, but rather only practical and concrete ones. A good example of clarity and succinctness in halachah is, "[A child should] not sit in his [father's] place, nor contradict him."

In this way, we gradually delegate responsibility to our children. They, in turn, don't accept the "bundle" of responsibility all at once, but instead, we allow for a period of adjustment after our explanation. This, in turn, is followed by integration and consolidation. Only afterwards does that particular behavior belong to the "obvious" category.

The Parental Presence

In order to properly fulfill our roles as *avi mori* and *imi morasi*, we must radiate our parental presence. That is, we must act in such a way that we transmit to our children the message that, "Ima is here and supports me whenever I need her; she guides me on the appropriate path and sets limits so that I won't lose my way, or stumble and fall." Abba wordlessly expresses, "I stand near you, my child—yes, a bit of a distance away to show you that I trust you and to allow you to function on your own within the parameters of that trust, and to allow you to practice and to accept responsibility. But I keep my eye on you from wherever I am. I remain on the lookout to make sure you don't stumble, yet I allow you to experience things and, through practice, to sharpen your skills so that you will be able to function independently throughout your life."

Sometimes our children resist parental authority and test us. At the same time, however, they transmit signs of relief when we know how to impose our authority. It is a kind of double message: "Don't do this to me…but please keep doing it!" In other words they are saying, "We find it difficult to obey, but your authority is important to us." We must acknowledge this message and be true to our role even when it seems to us that our children are having a hard time in accepting our authority.

Moreover, our children are not looking for a friend in their parents. Instead, they want an *av moreh* and an *ima morah*. Even when they grow up, even when they reach old age, they will always want to sense their parents' authority and lean on it. A child who senses that his parents do not set limits because they are weak may seem temporarily calm when he receives what he wants in the short term. Inside, however, he fears that there is no one stronger than he who can protect him and look after him. These fears can sometimes even cause him to go to extremes in undisciplined behavior, in order to force wishy-washy parents to come to their senses and insist on the limits that will give their child true confidence and peace.

We must remember that parental authority is the ability to determine appropriate paths for our children and to prevent them from doing things that hurt themselves or others. Authority does not mandate a show of force for its imposition, nor does it require immediate response in the face of disobedience. The opposite it true: it is only a weak parent who feels impelled to make a show of force, while one who is confident in his parenting abilities can take time out for deliberation when a child breaks the rules. Parental aura and authority do not require force. The use of force is, paradoxically, the result of a lack of authority.

Let us examine our parental profile: is each one of its components clear and directed? Do we use each in the correct balance? And especially, do we constantly daven for *siyatta diShmaya* to succeed in our task?

Tasty Morsels

A mother must grasp the "parental steering wheel" on two sides: with one hand—she must lead and direct, and with the other hand—she must stroke, encourage, and pacify.

Every child occasionally experiences bouts of tension and stubbornness. Try to soften the situation by giving the child a choice of two desirable options, such as, "Which shirt do you prefer—the blue one or the checked one?"

During a power struggle with your child, try to disarm him by keeping calm; your child will imitate you and your approach. Let's say he loudly demands, "I want ice cream before lunch!" In a quiet and serene tone of voice, you can answer him, "In our family, we receive ice cream at the end of the meal."

Give your child a coin to place in the tzedakah box after shopping at a local grocery store, to teach him to remember to give to the needy when he buys something for himself.

The warmth and tenderness we bestow on our children will never go astray, but will accompany them until old age and grant them the strength to

cope with the situations they encounter in life.

If you need to borrow a few coins from your child's pocket money (for bus fare, tzedakah, etc.), cite a date when you will return the money, and return the loan on time.

When we tell our children, "Let's consult on this important matter with Bubby and Zaidy," we are educating them to fulfill the command, "Ask your father and he will inform you, your elders and they will tell you" (*Devarim* 32:7).

Instead of arguing with a "selfish" two-year-old, say, "This is yours, but you can also allow others to play with it." When you are giving something to all your children, emphasize to your toddler, "This—belongs to everyone, and this—is yours." When a small child is sure about his share, he will accept the fact that others are also entitled to receive.

When you see Jews desecrating Shabbos, you can rouse your children to daven for "*tinokos she-nishbu*."

Encourage your children to manage a *gemach* of books or games for the other children in the neighborhood, and to contribute a book or game of their own occasionally. If such a *gemach* already exists, have them contribute a book or game of their own occasionally.

Ask your children to say their *berachos* out loud to give you the opportunity to say Amen. Let them answer Amen to your *berachos* as well.

Accustom your child to answer Amen when someone blesses him.

Make a habit of counting to ten in a whisper before responding to any unusual or disobedient action.

Anyone who plants a sapling knows not to dig in the flowerpot at frequent intervals to check if the plant has taken root. Instead we wait patiently until one fine day, we are pleasantly surprised to see that a flower has bloomed.

It is important to teach the child to use the word No toward herself as well: to say No to her *yetzer ha-ra*; even to shout out loud, "No, absolutely not!" during moments of trial and temptation.

Before leaving to go shopping or do errands, make a list together with your children.

Even when a baby asks for something, we can occasionally say, "Just a moment." He will learn to be patient, and his brothers and sisters will be gratified as well.

Food for thought: We thaw ice with warmth, not with the blows of a hammer. So, too, with emotional iciness and

apathy—warmth is the best solution.

It's a nice idea to send your child to a lonely neighbor or a sick acquaintance with a dish or a cake *lichvod Shabbos*, and a letter.

Teach your children to keep the stairwell and yard as clean as they keep the house itself.

View your home as an enterprise headed by you, the parents. Try to motivate the "household staff" out of interest and drive. When there is a lot of housework to be done, list the necessary household tasks for your children; each child will be happier carrying out the job that he or she chooses.

You, too, as the CEO of the enterprise, can also occasionally extend a helping hand to your workers, and if you hum a song as you do so, the atmosphere in your home will improve unrecognizably.

Let us strengthen our relationship with Bubby and Zaidy. From time to time, send a cake or a bouquet of flowers with a grandchild to Bubby, *lichvod Shabbos*. Prepare a small surprise for Zaidy with the help of the children. For example, we can encourage our daughter to call her Zaidy out of the blue, and recount an anecdote from her daily life.

Suggest that your child write a letter to someone, perhaps a relative who lives in a different city or country. If he doesn't yet know how to write, take "dictation" and record his words. Try to save a copy of the letter to show your child later, when he knows how to read.

Let your child select a candy or game from a variety of options. This way, you are helping her develop good judgment and the ability to choose.

How many times a day does a baby hear that he or she is loved, and from numerous family members? Continue the same custom for a three-year-old, a nine-year-old and even a fourteen-year-old child and beyond. It is important that they, too, hear that they are loved.

When a parent *initiates giving to* his child, this will encourage the child to be satisfied. When the child *initiates taking from* his parents, he is likely to want more and more.

When you need a break to daven or rest, suggest some kind of pleasant activity to your child that you set aside especially for this time.

Inquire if there is a sick child in your child's class. Encourage your child to call the sick child and ask how he feels, even if he is not one of his close friends.

It is important to repeat the following to our children until they learn it by heart: "To Ima and Abba you can tell everything, but you can't tell everything to everyone else."

When your children sit together on one bench, try to show them that when each one moves *a little*, they clear *a lot* of space for an additional person.

When your children see you preparing packages of nice clothing in good condition to contribute to the needy, take advantage of the excellent opportunity to teach them about gracious giving.

When we encounter a brick wall that blocks our educational path, let's not bang our heads against it. Instead, let us bypass it and search for alternate routes to advance toward our goal.

When you play competitive games with your children, choose occasionally not to win. This can be an opportunity to show children how to cope gracefully with losing.

Learn, and teach your children, how to take advantage of leftovers. Consult with your children by asking, "What can we do with this dish?" This way, you demonstrate how to avoid *bal tashchis*.

Try to serve food to the family

in a central platter, in order to teach family members how to be considerate of others.

A lovely habit to get into: after each person washes *netilas yadayim* for a meal, he or she fills the cup with water for the next in line.

Your child is capable of listening, obeying, and learning only when he is emotionally available. When a child is angry, afraid, or sad, he is not open to receiving direction or advice.

Do you suspect that you are more "*morasi*" to your Rivki, and less "*imi*"? Play a tape recorder when she is with you, and then analyze the situation when you listen to the tape later, alone.

Encourage your children to recite the chapters of *mishnayos* that they've learned by heart to their Zaidy. He will be happy, and Bubby will get much *nachas* as well.

Encourage your children to send something by mail to a brother or a cousin in yeshiva—perhaps a warmhearted note that they write themselves.

When your son comes home from yeshiva, remember that he wants to fill his heart with the feelings of "Home Sweet Home"—from home-cooked delicacies and cakes to catching up on family news.

רות

Encourage his brothers and sisters to join you in bringing him back into the family loop.

In times of trouble as well as joy, let us accustom our children to giving tzedakah. When we give in times of distress we can add a prayer for *refuah* and *yeshuah* to the individual and the *klal*. When we give in times of happiness, we can add a prayer of thanksgiving to Hashem for His great kindness to us.

You surely love your children a great deal, but remember that it is important for them to *hear it from you frequently, at every age*. In order to remind each of your children of your love at every opportunity, try to fill your pockets with "Vitamin Ima," and dispense liberally to each of your kids. Here are some examples:

~ "When you run around having fun, it makes me happy to see your adorable peyos fluttering happily in the breeze."

~ "I'll tell you a secret—your Ima loves you!"

~ "Your beauty mark really adds a lot of beauty to you."

~ "Do you want to know what I feel? Joy in my heart that you, Motti, are my child."

~ Ask your daughter, "Why do you think I love you?" After

she brings up her ideas, tell her your opinion: "That, too—but the most important reason that I love you is because you're my daughter!"

~ Pat your child's hand and say, "Yasher koach!" When your children come home, greet them by saying, "Welcome!", "Shalom aleichem!", "I'm so glad you're home!" Look straight into your child's eyes with a warm, loving gaze.

You can prepare the younger ones for your absence via puppet games; encourage them to express their thoughts and feelings.

How can we teach our children to give others *kaf zechus*, the benefit of the doubt? Tell them about a scenario that took place, or even an imaginary but probable one, and try to analyze the situation together while finding a *zechus* for those involved.

Some children are better at describing their thoughts and wishes in writing. Encourage them to do so.

When you know you will have to be away from home for a period of time, prepare your children in advance. Involve them in what will take place while you're away, talk to them, and listen. If you will be away from home for a few days, a calendar will demonstrate the passing days to the children. Suggest that they place a sticker over each passing day on the calendar—this will ease their expectations and longings.

It is advisable to dedicate time and thought to gathering "personal information" about each one of our children: needs, abilities, difficulties, communication style, etc. When we turn to Yossi we speak clearly and briefly, but Esti needs more detailed explanations. This information is important and useful in educating each child "*al pi darko*," according to his nature (*Mishlei* 131:2).

When you are sensitive to your child's needs and are proactive in fulfilling them, your child feels like one who has *pas b'salo*, one whose basic needs are met and has no need to be demanding. Offer to read your children a story at bedtime; take into account that Avreimi prefers yeast cakes and that Miri collects stationery.

2
The Inborn Encouragement Tool Kit

Every parent knows that encouragement and support are two important resources used by parents to raise and educate their children. Thus, parents ask themselves occasionally, "How much encouragement does my child need? How can I, as a parent, support my child effectively?

When we really stop and think about the issue, we discover that the answers are to be found within ourselves. Some of us are simply not aware of our own powers and capabilities. Sometimes we attempt to learn how to acquire these skills when, in fact, we latently possess them. In fact, we can call the wonderful abilities that HaKadosh Baruch Hu has granted us our "individualized parental tool kit." This kit is stocked full of diverse and varied tools, and it is wonderful indeed to discover that we naturally employ these tools in the right doses and at the right times.

Encouragement Facilitates Progress from Childhood until Old Age

Let us track the development of an infant's first year. No mother would expect a baby to accomplish a feat that she instinctively knows he is not capable of performing. For example, she will not urge a six-month-old to walk nor offer him stimulation in order to speed up his ambulatory development. Walking represents a stage of development that must take place in its proper time, and the parents' level of expectation is instinctively geared to this.

When a baby does reach the appropriate age to start walking, the parents wait for signs from the child that signal her developmental readiness. Then, when the baby does extend a wobbly foot forward, her mother immediately stands opposite her with shining eyes, extending her arms out to her and encouraging her to continue. Perhaps her encouraging words and tone will inspirit the baby to extend her other foot forward… or perhaps she won't dare. Either way, when the mother stands before her baby, her body language makes it clear that she has no intention of pushing the child; she simply wants to face her and support her if she should need her.

A mother's behavior toward her toddler teaches us an appropriate and beneficial parental response to children even during later stages of development. How encouraging and inviting it is for a child to progress when his parents face him in an inviting pose, their faces turned toward him with excitement and acceptance!

In our initial interaction with our baby, we seem to possess the instinctive understanding that each baby develops at his or her own pace. Our expectations, then, are geared to our specific baby as he unfolds according to the manner that is appropriate to his unique pace. For example, a mother will stand before her toddler at a distance of a single step. She won't distance herself four steps because she knows that her baby will take one step, not four, the very first time. This simple understanding has invaluable significance. The expectation of one step at a time is a healthy one. There is no point in expecting children to go against their developmental readiness and attempt to bypass the natural process and surpass their abilities in one fell swoop!

When we analyze the image of the mother standing opposite her infant, we see that her pose and body language all convey encouragement. She does not stand straight and command the baby to walk; instead, she stands a little bent over and communicates her absolute readiness to accept him in her arms at the moment that he will need her. Her arms are extended to him and her entire body resonates with acceptance. Her inviting facial expression reflects delightful anticipation and her words are both compelling and supportive.

These finely tuned insights and distinctions are taken from the "inborn encouragement tool kit" that HaKadosh Baruch Hu has bestowed on all parents. Note we mothers' response to our baby's first step when it finally takes place. On one hand we are pleased and even express our joy; our baby will surely discern this in our facial expression and through the pleasant noises we make. On the other hand we are careful not to make loud, raucous noises, so as not to frighten the baby or hasten him to fall.

This intuitive understanding of a balanced reaction remains with us when the infant grows into a child, a youngster, and then an adolescent. One day he returns from school with a high grade on an exam. Exaggerated applause by us, the parents, may cause him to worry if his parents will accept him if he doesn't bring home high grades the next time. Thus, our instinctive caution, which accompanied our response to the infant, is appropriate for the older child as well. Too much ado concerning the child's achievements may deter him, since over-encouragement or exaggerated praise is sometimes intimidating.

After the toddler's first step, parents naturally encourage the next one. If the second step is delayed for some reason, it would never occur to parents to get angry and "accuse" the toddler for not taking two steps. They would never say, "Why do you take only one step and not two?" His one step satisfies us at this stage. We are not disappointed and do not prod the toddler to express his physical capabilities before he is ready.

If we are wise enough to praise our ten-year-old daughter for cleaning up, and to tell her how pleasant it is to walk into the kitchen—even if her efforts are not exactly up to our standards—she will want to do it again in the future, and will try to do an even more thorough job the next time. Of course, we have no guarantee that the next step will transpire in the very near future and bring about significant progress. We must not forget that *every step—even the smallest—brings us closer to our goal, and it is important to appreciate even minor "baby steps" in the proper direction.*

Let us imagine the case of a child who often hits his brothers but due to special efforts on the part of his mother, he refrains from hitting on two separate occasions. Even though he continues to hit his brothers afterwards, the two isolated cases of self-control can be a springboard for true change—if his parents will be wise enough to notice these efforts and appreciate them.

Sometimes a baby stumbles and falls when he tries to take his first step. How much empathy and understanding does he merit to receive! His parents pick him up and encourage him to try again out of absolute confidence in his abilities, despite his present misstep. Clearly, no one asks the baby, "Why did you fall?! How awful!" Instead, we identify with the baby's sorrow and comfort him by stroking and hugging him. This is exactly what we mean by encouragement.

What happens with an older child? He, too, may stumble and fall. But the older child's "misstep" may be a punishment he received in school, for example. A comforting and empathetic response, together with educational guidance, will give him the strength to overcome this unpleasant hindrance and forge on with hope. Our responses can imbue our children with the confidence they need to take the next step without fear. *We remain at our children's sides in case they should stumble, and when they do fall we assist them and teach them how to transform their stumbling blocks into building blocks.*

Our intention is not to allow our children to do whatever they want. However, there is great significance to the initial stance and attitude that we adopt when we guide our children in order to correct and improve their behavior. *A comment made to a child from a position of patience and acceptance will be received on a more positive note than the same comment that is voiced out of anger, frustration, and shame.* Our reactions while we place limits on and guide our children will enable them to change in a positive direction—as long as our efforts stem from a place of forgiveness that is devoid of anger.

Using Encouragement

As parents, we are well aware of our ultimate goals. With the birth of every baby, we are showered with blessings by others to raise our child to Torah, chuppah, and *ma'asim tovim* (good deeds). Our ultimate goal is to bring our child to become a faithful *oved Hashem*, servant of God. In practice, however, our daily lives are filled with routine, mundane tasks. Yet we must make an effort to remember that these thoroughly unheroic tasks do, indeed, contribute to our children's spiritual progress and bring them closer to actualizing our ultimate goals.

The inborn and ready-made encouragement tool kit—which is latent in each and every parent—helps us to succeed in our opera-

tional goals. We can use the gift of encouragement throughout each stage of childhood. Encouragement includes our warm welcome of each progressive developmental step, reinforcement in the face of failure, emotional identification together with a firm grasp of the child's actual abilities, and an attitude that does not demand more than is appropriate yet advances the child and calls on him to stride forward according to his own way—and, *b'ezras Hashem*, to grow and flourish.

Give your child the opportunity to enjoy his own successes. Offer him a challenge that he can overcome successfully, and when he does fulfill the task praise and cheer him on sincerely. Thus you will instill in your child a belief in his own abilities and the readiness to cope with challenges.

Personal experience is the best way to learn. It is important to restrain oneself from criticizing a child in the face of failure, and to give her the opportunity to experiment and experience things on her own.

Instead of criticizing, direct the child to improve. Instead of saying, "Why did you spill your drink?" it is better to say, "We only drink when we sit down next to the table."

Sometimes we must admonish or rebuke a child for something serious he has done. He knows that he was out of line and suffers pangs of conscience. He may worry that we will love him less for it. Therefore it is important, even during periods of anger and rebuke, that we make it clear to our child that he is loved and wanted despite everything.

A child makes a mistake, a child stumbles or fails. We can simply say, "Oy, what a shame!"

When you feed your baby, try occasionally to allow him to make the effort to stretch his head to the spoon.

Even positive labels can burden the child and limit his activities. It is hard for a child to have to live up to the label of the "diligent child" or "studious one" in the family. Sometimes the child even feels in the depths of his heart that he does not live up to his reputation!

It is good for a child to live in a home whose members can talk about failures and mistakes freely, and where the child finds an open ear and support that enables him to gather the strength to overcome and cope with obstacles.

Let us try to make our children aware that we love them with *ahavas chinam*—unconditional love, absolute love that does not depend on specific behavior. This kind of love has the power to arouse the child's desire to improve and correct her behavior.

Encouragement is expressed not only in words but mainly in facial expressions. Look at your child with a direct, warm, and content gaze, nod your head to show your agreement, and let your demeanor express sincere appreciation.

Tell your child how you coped with failures in the past.

A two-year-old wants to get dressed on his own? Make time for him to try to get dressed on his own, under your direction.

Make an effort to accept your children's help cheerfully and happily, even if the results are not perfect.

When you make the time for quality, one-on-one attention, your child will sense your support and will relax. Sitting close to the child, listening actively, maintaining an attentive expression and an interested gaze, and expressing brief vocal responses such as "Oh, my," "Hmm..." or "I see" will all convey your honest desire to share with your child and show how much you really care about him.

Encourage children who are learning to read by writing them short letters and putting these notes in envelopes with their names on them.

When our expectation level for our child is too high and unrealistic, we start to feel disappointed and bitter toward him in the face of his failures. He, in turn, will also be disappointed in himself and despair of ever earning our praise. But an appropriate level of expectation will help give the child encouragement and kindness, as well as the strength to try over and over again.

After a child has successfully overcome his *yetzer ha-ra*, it's important to demonstrate to him the sweet taste of satisfaction after restraint. You can say, "Don't you feel so happy that you controlled yourself from hitting your baby brother?" or "You must feel so proud of yourself that you sat down and finished all your homework."

Do you want to strengthen desirable behavior and, at the same time, encourage sibling unity? Allow your children to accumulate "mitzvah points" as a group in a joint fund. A pre-determined number of these points will entitle them to a prize, either a group prize or an individual prize for each child.

The night before a child has an exam, write a small encouraging note and insert it into his or her backpack such as, "To Sarah, my 'right hand'—Good luck!" or "Moishi—By me, you're always a '100'!"

Sur me-ra va'aseh tov—"Turn from evil and do good" (*Tehillim* 34:15). A child who has stumbled and fallen first needs support and encouragement in order to pick himself up. Then he needs admonishment in order to *sur me-ra*, turn from evil. After that, he needs guidance in order to learn how to *aseh tov*, do good.

Avoid labeling a child in light of negative behavior. If you say, "You always forget your homework," he will despair of ever changing. Relate only to the act itself—forgetting the homework—and do not criticize the child's character as a result—by calling him irresponsible, for example.

Let us relate to a child's actions and describe them without "crowning" him with labels and titles. As a result, he will learn which actions are proper and which are not. For example, if you see one of the children picking up a candy wrapper from the floor and throwing it into the trash can, instead of saying, "Wow! What a little tzaddik you are!" you can say, "Wow! You saw a wrapper and cared enough to put it into the trash can. What a great thing to do!" After hearing a commendation such as this, the child will give himself a "crown."

When you receive positive reports about a child from the nursery school teacher, the homeroom teacher or the rebbe, tell your child as well as Abba.

The "language of the heart" is very powerful. If we sincerely believe in a child's strengths and abilities, we can succeed in transmitting, in nonverbal ways, the message that he or she is qualified and capable.

A child hits his younger brother? Rebuke him, then add a hug or smile.

Find opportunities to guide your children in various tasks they might perform in the future, in a constructive, matter-of-fact, and non-critical manner: the proper way to wash dishes, how to organize their bedroom, and even the proper way to take out the garbage.

Constructive praise should contain two elements: the facts and their benefits. Describe what you see, and the positive emotions it causes. For example: "You gave your brother a toy and you calmed him down. I am happy to see that," "It's wonderful to see a child who offers his own candy to his brothers," "I enjoyed seeing what you did."

3

The Family Meeting

WE ARE ALL FAMILIAR with the uplifting family gathering around the Shabbos table, where the *neshamah yeseirah* and *kedushah* of Shabbos are tangibly felt. However, proper functioning of the family enterprise also necessitates weekday gatherings or meetings for discussion of various topics that need attention within the family framework. These "family happy hours," which take place on a regular weekday, are most satisfying if accompanied by tasty refreshments in a relaxed atmosphere of cooperation and acceptance.

Areivus

The family is an all-encompassing, cohesive unit that unites its members and makes them responsible for one another. Family members are untied under the banner of *areivus*. There are three facets to the concept of *areivus*, which combined make up its meaning.

The first is **involvement**. Links in a chain are intertwined with one another. When one link is moved, the rest of them follow suit. Family members are intertwined in much the same way so that a change in the situation of one is likely to cause movement and change in the lives of the others.

The second is **responsibility**. Family members are responsible for one another. When a ship is in danger of sinking, each and every passenger must work to preserve the entire ship and not just his or her own cabin. Similarly, each and every family member is required to shoulder some of the responsibility of the family and preserve the family's unity for the welfare of all the members.

The third is the sweet taste of **family togetherness** that wise parents know how to instill in their children. This sweetness and pleasantness will preserve familial ties over many, many years.

Goals and Objectives

The objective of the family gathering is to strengthen the feeling of *areivus* by affording each member the opportunity to be heard and hear others, two actions that unify the family. This is the time for family members to talk about their experiences, to discuss issues that bother them, and to inform the others of important matters and occurrences as well as future plans in the upcoming days. Each member is invited to update the others as well as tell about private experiences that he or she chooses to share. It is important, for the sake of family unity, to listen, to empathize with, and to try to understand the other. Each family member should manifest his interest in the others at the meeting. Each person has his or her needs, together with the joint need to create togetherness in the home

The family gathering is the time and the place for family empowerment; it affords children the opportunity to transmit and absorb the strength of the family in a directed, planned manner. It engenders true friendships, with the goal of strengthening overall familial camaraderie and closeness. Even in families where there are many physical and verbal provocations among siblings, the family "happy hour" has the power to unify and unite, to arouse brotherhood and friendship. We highly recommend that you actively initiate these meetings.

Decorum and Topics

The authoritative parental presence must be evident in this meeting, as parents represent leadership in the home. We can channel the conversation in the family meeting around important or happy events that happened in the past, or are scheduled to take place in the future, to one or more family members. While listening actively, we open up to emotions and not only to facts. The emotional connection lends depth to the interpersonal relationships.

Sitting together also allows room for bringing up negative experiences—sad, disappointing, and worrisome events. A child who experienced a setback or failure in school will find a sympathetic ear, and family members will encourage him to express his negative emotions surrounding the experience. Parents can and should direct children to express themselves cautiously and carefully so that they will know how to portray even disturbing events in an appropriate way.

Another issue to be taken up in family meetings is mutual assistance and sharing of the family load. "Next week, we start two weeks of tests in my seminary," a daughter might tell her family members. "I'm afraid that I won't be able to take care of my regular chores around the house during this time period. Who can switch with me

for these two weeks?" "On Thursday I have an appointment with the eye doctor," the mother updates the family. "What will be with the Shabbos baking?" Together, we coordinate how the family will mobilize itself to help one another. This kind of "working communication" creates an environment of giving and taking, helping and being helped in turn. Sometimes we can also allow our children to express complaints, while making sure that these do not cross the boundaries of appropriate behavior and attitudes.

Plan and Content for the Meeting

A pleasant joint activity can be an excellent backdrop for a meeting. You can prepare a family quiz for a few minutes, family members can tell jokes, or someone can repeat a short, interesting story that she heard during the week. It might be fun to hear what Yossi wants to be when he grows up, or the ambitions and wishes of other family members. These activities open up the lines of communication, creating an atmosphere of candidness that reaches down to deeper layers of the soul that do not often find expression in daily life.

The family meeting is an excellent venue for parents to accomplish their own childrearing goals. We can gently transmit social and educational messages such as: How can I continue to speak nicely even when someone is hurting me? What do I say to my brother when something about his behavior bothers me? How can I explain myself without hurting the other person, and how can I listen—but really listen—to other people? We can also use something that happened during the week to transmit an educational message. For example, Ima can describe how she saw a group of children harassing an unfortunate child at the bus stop, and ask her own children how one should treat such a situation. Acquiring these social skills specifically via the parents contributes a great deal to family ties.

Take advantage of the family meeting to update the children about what is happening at home. When children are kept abreast of events on the calendar they are much more likely to show concern and extend a helping hand. “Tomorrow, baby Chaim’ke will be getting a shot, and he may get a high fever as a result.” In light of this information, children will be considerate of their mother when they see her the morning after the vaccination, looking tired and bleary-eyed. They will understand, without being told, that she did not sleep much last night because she was busy with the baby, and will not worry when they hear Chaim’ke cry during the night. This is only one example of how to prepare children for an upcoming event.

Try to involve your children in suggestions and decisions when appropriate, such us, "Let's think of a plan together for an outdoor family outing during one of the days of vacation." The parents should be the ones to lead this discussion.

Many families have sons learning in *yeshivos* who cannot attend family meetings regularly. Don't forget them. Remember to tell, or write them, about the latest meeting, and about any special news and any decisions that were reached.

You can also take use family meetings for preparatory briefings before the holidays to plan your shopping or to create a work-plan for family members that will include one-time tasks as well as regular chores for a specified period of time—such as cleaning in the weeks before Pesach. It's a good idea to draw up the work-plan on a blackboard or poster and allot a prominent place for it in the home. This is a golden opportunity to transmit the concept of *areivus* to the children. Those who think that chores belong only in the mother's domain will be happy to discover their own meaningful share of household responsibilities. This will engender concern and sensitivity, which will result in their taking the initiative in home economics. This way, the family will approach the Yom Tov with a spirit of mutual help and a feeling of togetherness, in which each member feels that he had a part in shouldering the general responsibility. This is how children learn to lend a hand together with their parents in household activities.

Inner Familial Empowerment in the Face of Negative Outside Influences

The family gathering also serves to consolidate the inner strength of the home. Although it is impossible to completely ward off external influences, family cohesiveness in a well-organized home bestows the stability that is so lacking in our times. The more the family is united around itself, and the more parents know exactly the direction they want to lead their ship, the more family members will be able to resist external temptations.

Children will bring to our attention what "everyone" does and what "everyone" buys: "All my friends get lots of money for Chanukah," they might say, or "On *Chol HaMoed*, everybody goes on trips," or "Everyone we know buys new clothes for Pesach; I also want a new outfit!" Family unity breaks up and curbs this pressure. Furthermore, parents who take the initiative and lead the family instead of allowing the family to be pulled by outside forces will always prepare

themselves and the home for what awaits them at the next bend in the road. These parents will know how to relate to external influences to which their children are exposed, and to build their home as a strong ship that sails safely though the stormy seas of life.

Parents who have family meetings on a regular basis report that these meetings strengthen cooperation and the sense of belonging to their great enterprise known as the family, which leads to the growth of desire to help one another—all with the support and guidance of the parents.

Tasty Morsels

The family meeting is the opportunity to sit together, to listen to and "sense" each member, and to relate to the family unit as a whole.

To encourage feelings of brotherhood during the family meeting, try to use statements such as the following and encourage others to sprinkle them liberally with their words as well: "In our house, we like it when…," "In our home, we are happy that…," "Ima feels happy when…," "I like being with my brother Shia because…," "When my sister Leah'le does _____, I feel happy," "In our family, it is important that…," "Our Abba and Ima are pleased when…," "This week I learned that it's not a good idea to do _____," "Thank you, Ima, for doing _____."

Allowing your imagination to carry you away a little when you're with your children helps you face reality better when you "come back down to earth." "What kind of work will you want to do when you will be an Abba?" "If you were a rebbe in a cheder, what would you do about _____ with your pupils?" "Let's pretend that you are a queen. What acts of *chessed* would you do with your vast treasures?" "Let's imagine Shifra'le in another thirty years."

Let us emphasize to our sons in cheder or talmud Torah how important their Torah learning is to the entire family, and how grateful we are to them for it. We can reserve family meetings, excursions and special activities to Rosh Chodesh when they come home early, and consult with them about which menu they prefer on Rosh Chodesh.

Here are some suggestions for the family gathering:

~ One of the parents describes an incident and how the people involved reacted. The children are asked to express their opinions about a specific behavior or explain how they would have acted under the same circumstances.

~ A short skit performed by the children or occasionally, for the purpose of variety, performed by Ima.

~ Tell a story and encourage the children to justify the actions of all the characters *lechaf zechus*.

~ Create a "progressive story": one of the children starts the first sentence and each person adds a sentence until a family story develops.

~ Set the following objective for the upcoming week: each

child should observe his brothers and sisters during the week and be prepared to describe one good deed performed by each one of them. This will engender positive feelings among all family members and will encourage the children to see the good in their fellowman.

~ Each child tells a short story on subjects such as, "A good deed my sister did," "How I avoided an argument with my brother," etc.

~ Draw a "family picture" in which everyone takes part: spread out a large roll of paper and have everyone draw something on it. When it's completed, be sure to hang it in the children's room where it will hang proudly, the product of family togetherness. Creative children will be happy to add a story to explain the picture.

~ Play party games. They're a lot of fun.

~ For younger children, try using a hand-puppet to instill educational messages in an enjoyable, experiential manner.

~ Pick a theme such as, "The satisfaction that comes from self-control," and describe it or tell a real story about it.

~ Create family songs, preferably composed and set to

music by family members, which relate to each individual child. It's a lot easier, and just as fun, to use a well-known melody.

Let us sit quietly with our children and listen intently to the sounds of our house and nearby surroundings: the ticking of a clock, hum of the refrigerator, chirping of birds, drizzling of rain, and whistling of the wind.

Take your children on guided tours: to the bakery, to the *arba'ah minim* shuk or store, to the *tefillin*-making workshop, and more. Prepare the children in advance of these tours.

Prepare together for a guest due to arrive shortly. Think together with the children how we can make his or her stay with us more pleasant.

An unusual idea for a family experience: study *pesukim* with the children that describe the sun, such as, "The sun is like a groom coming out from his bridal canopy" (*Tehillim* 19:6)—and then take the children to watch the sunrise.

You will find it fascinating to ask your children, "What memories do you like to recall?" "What wouldn't you ever want to forget?" or "What would you prefer to forget?"

A lovely method to go over the

Taryag (six hundred and thirteen) mitzvos: the children sit in a circle and each child in turn adds a *mitzvas aseh* and *mitzvas lo sa'aseh*.

Collect and save the endearing notes your children write you. On the back of each one, write the date it was written and under what circumstances. Then, as the years go by, take the opportunity to look them over occasionally with your children.

Here's an idea for sibling togetherness: the children sit together and listen to a story that one child reads out loud. Bubby can also read an engrossing story to the children in serialized form; she reads one chapter during each visit. (You will also enjoy sitting and listening in occasionally.)

An interesting activity during the family meeting: each participant reveals an activity that he or she would like to do with Ima, with Abba, with his older brother, with her younger sister, etc.

4 The Family Atmosphere

WHAT HAPPENS TO ALL the words, sentences and statements that are uttered in our households over the years? Where do they disappear to, after they are articulated? It would seem that our speech has a very short life span, and that our words disappear into thin air immediately after they are uttered. But that's not necessarily the case. Each of us can recall words that resonate in our ears for hours and days, and sometimes even expressions that remain engraved in our memories for years afterwards.

Many of our inner voices (things we think to ourselves) are taken from the atmosphere of our own childhood home. Listening to these voices will help us identify the magnitude and significance of the lessons a child absorbs via what is said and done in the home, as well as enable us to figure out which inner voices we want to cultivate in our children's psyches and souls.

The Very Walls of a Person's Home Bear Witness to Him

The very walls of our houses absorb statements. If we could make them come alive, what would they reveal? Perhaps we would be able to distinguish a number of different types of statements, for example, the regular use of *Shem Shamayim* in our speech ("*Baruch Hashem*!", "*Im yirtzeh Hashem*," "*B'ezras Hashem*"). Perhaps there would be another category that includes expressions relating to the pace of our daily activities, such as, "Hurry up! We have to get going." Another type might be composed of appeals and demands we have of household members, their requests of us and our responses to them: "Please wash the dishes now," or "May I have another lollipop?" "No, but you can have one after supper."

Air and Atmosphere

Atmosphere is similar to the air we breathe. The air is made up of everything we inhale and exhale; it is the sum total of the air after it is processed by each one of the people who breathe it. The family "air" or atmosphere also represents the totality of everything that is found, and takes place, in the home—and every family member affects it and is affected by it. The atmosphere is influenced by dates

and events: there is a special atmosphere on erev Shabbos, on Yom Tov and at a joyous family gathering, and there may also be a more subdued ambiance during pain or illness, God forbid. The home atmosphere is created from pleasant happenings as well as unpleasant ones. It is always present.

Parents "exhale" both overt and subliminal messages that are "inhaled" and absorbed by their children, who then mold their worldview and aspirations around these messages. Children absorb not only words but facial expressions and body language, together with additional visual and sensory elements. Together, they forge the breeding ground for the way the child views himself, his environment, and the entire world, as well as forms his motives for choosing his actions.

The home atmosphere is where the child "breathes in" his first encounter with values and their prioritization. The home teaches the child—sometimes unintentionally—what is important and what is not, what is bad and what is good, what we value and whom we value, what is essential and what is only enjoyable, what elicits a response and what is self-understood, what excites us and what leaves us apathetic, what makes us happy and what makes us frightened.

Within the home atmosphere, we criticize X… or we accept Y and guide her. We blame X… or we accept responsibility for Y. The atmosphere comprises the whole. Together we anticipate and are disappointed, we honor and we scorn, we complain about X, we are satisfied with Y. Some things make us happy and others make us sad. We worry about X, and are encouraged by Y. Either we tend to see the half-full cup, or are liable to see the half-empty one. We can demand from others, or we can appeal to them with a graceful request. We avoid the evil, or actively pursue the good; we criticize or encourage.

Furthermore, we also learn from the family environment how we are to react to the constraints of life: with grumbling and impatience, or with acceptance and serenity. We learn that when life gives us lemons, we can complain… or we can make lemonade. All acquired human traits are molded by the family atmosphere.

An atmosphere of open communication in the home also has ramifications for the child such as: can the child share his emotions in the home, both feelings of joy as well as those of pain and distress? In our home, do we feel the pain of another's failure? Is there room for questions, even "unorthodox" ones? Does our home environment support and promote basic, mutual interest in each other? What is our worldview regarding money, education and personal abilities?

Parents Shape the Family Atmosphere

As the home is the source and very basis for producing one's worldview, parents who succeed in coping with challenges in their lives will be able to better guide their children in coping with the latter's own personal issues. Thus, a great responsibility toward their families rests on parents, because children learn how to approach life and choose their outlook from watching how their parents respond to life's vicissitudes.

A child sees how the parent responds to the important things going on in the parent's life, and she imitates this. She absorbs within herself how her parent functions as a daughter, sister, or friend, as a neighbor or employee, and thus in all of life's domains.

We must recognize the great influence we have as parents over our children's choices. True, there are many factors that influence our children, and many that we cannot control. We can only demand of ourselves to be alert to those actions of ours that may affect our children's actions. Ultimately, we are not masters of what our child chooses to do with his life, yet we should take responsibility for what we *can* contribute, and pray that Hashem will take over from there.

A child is more inclined to internalize educational lessons when observing his parents' actions regarding *their* personal issues. Shimi comes home from school angry and frustrated. He grumbles to his mother that he lent a pencil to a friend, and the friend sharpened the pencil so much that it was returned to him at half of its original size. "Why do you allow such nonsense to get you down?" Shimi's mother responds. "You should be happy that you had the privilege to do a *chessed* for someone!"

Half an hour passes, and a neighbor knocks on the door to borrow a hand mixer from Ima. The neighbor returns it later, but not as clean as Ima had hoped it would be. What does Shimi's mother say? "This is how she returns something she borrows? She didn't even try to wash it properly!" Shimi heard only a short time ago that he should be happy at the opportunity to do a *chessed*, but this is not the message he will retain. His mother's response to *her own* issue—the state of her mixer—is the real message he will internalize. Words are important, but actions speak louder than words. The child will imitate his parent's actions, especially those that stem from what affected the parent personally. It will be powerful indeed when parents express forgiveness and leniency to others in issues that are important to them.

A child acquires a worldview in his home not only concerning values, but vis-à-vis rules, regulations and habits of daily life as well: how important it is to get up early in the morning, to get enough sleep, to take rests and respites, and to make appropriate use of time. The child internalizes what is accepted and what is not from the norms in his home: whether a nap in the afternoon is a self-understood need or is viewed as laziness, whether a cleaning lady is a necessary expense or is considered an indulgence. And when cleaning the house, what is considered to be adequate? Do we do a thorough, major cleaning once a week, once a month, or less frequently?

Even our attitudes toward a healthy body, nutrition and medicine are affected by the worldview we imbibe in our childhood home. Sometimes they are formed because of the family's approach and sometimes despite it—but always under the home's influence.

The Value of Togetherness

The home atmosphere should bestow on family members the strong sense that they are part and parcel of a loving, supportive family. This feeling accompanies the child wherever she turns and gives her the strength to cope and overcome problems in every situation. But family togetherness does not necessarily materialize on its own: it must be created and nurtured, and we must invest thought in how to strengthen it.

Statements that Accompany the Child through Life

The "air" of the home is replete with statements and declarations that will accompany family members for the rest of their lives. Many of these statements penetrate the soul and wait there for the appropriate time. When they are needed, they rise to the surface to calm us with their wisdom: "I'm responsible for effort; the results are in Hashem's hands," "Even a tiny positive gesture can have huge repercussions," "You can't get everything you need, and you don't need everything you can get."

The child will hear significant statements such as these within the home environment in different contexts. When he behaves in a way that exemplifies one of them, take advantage of this opportunity to explain its significance.

When the time comes, a child will attach the familiar statement to something that happens to him, and suddenly the principle embodied in the proverb or saying will illuminate his path in life. This sudden realization flows from the reservoir created by the family atmosphere.

Our Generation and Previous Generations: *Toras Imecha*

How were our mothers, in past generations, able to instill pure *yiras Shamayim* in their homes, *yiras Shamayim* that emanated from pure, unadulterated *emunah* divorced from intellectual gymnastics? Why is it that precisely in our educated and enlightened generation, true fear of Heaven has atrophied in so many hearts?

When we take a close look at previous generations, we realize that the Jewish mother breathed Godliness into the very air of her home: her closeness to the Ribbono shel Olam was expressed in the caretaking of her children and in her housework. She would turn to the Master of the universe and talk to Him as a daughter speaks to her father, imploring Him to let her children grow up healthy and strong in order to worship their Creator. "Ribbono shel Olam" when changing a diaper, and "Ribbono shel Olam" while stirring her soup on the stove. In short, *Shem Shamayim* was always on her lips throughout the entire day.

The child spends most of his day with his mother, especially during his early years. His very senses absorb his mother's closeness with our merciful Father in Heaven as expressed in her appeals to Him for every need and desire. The child internalizes this dependence on Hashem and the understanding that everything originates from Him when he hears his mother's requests. "I beseech you, Merciful Father, inspire my husband and sons with your holy Torah," or even, "Please, Ribbono shel Olam, let me merit to make all the beds in this house this morning" (in other words, that there shouldn't be sick children who remain in bed all day).

Children learn constant thanksgiving to the Creator of the world from their mothers as they hear her repeat, "*Baruch Hashem*," "Thank God," or "*Gott tzu dank*." Even a small child absorbs his mother's humility in the face of God's benevolence, the "*katonti mi-kol ha-chassadim*"—the attitude that we are undeserving of Hashem's kindness. This awareness of our own paltry abilities next to Hashem's highlights our obligations in the face of His benevolence and provides the very foundations for the child's service of Hashem, which he acquires while still a toddler and small child.

And then, when a boy or girl goes to school and begins to learn Chumash, they encounter the name of Hashem from their rebbe or teacher: the Name which has already become so familiar to them from their mother at home, the great and awesome Creator of the world. The seeds which have been so carefully planted in their minds will find the cultivated and fertile soil of *emunah* in their hearts, soil that is ready to absorb the new seedlings.

The Family Atmosphere as a Strengthening Force

Bringing Godliness into our homes in a way that our children can understand is an excellent way to endear *Shem Shamayim* to their hearts. They will breathe *Shem Shamayim* between the walls of our homes, according to the tradition of our mothers throughout the generations. Especially in our own times, when children are continuously threatened by exposure to difficult and frightening events, we as parents must make every effort to strengthen their *emunah* as a bulwark against misfortune. When parents respond with *emunah* and *bitachon* during difficult times, children absorb the all-important message, "O Yisrael, trust in the Eternal; their help and their shield is He!" They learn that reliance on Hashem is what brings salvation, and that Hashem will not abandon His nation: "For the Eternal will not forsake His people" (*Tehillim* 115:9, 94:14).

During trying times, we must take special care to suffuse the family atmosphere with stories of Hashem's *hashgachah*, about trust and *bitachon* in Hashem, about the importance of *Am Yisrael* and the great future that awaits us. This abundance of "*emunah*-talk" will furnish answers to questions before they are even asked, and fill us with strength to stand firm in our faith when coping with the trials of life.

Close your eyes and recall a pleasant memory from your parent's home…and then try to think: What pleasant memories will my children be likely to recall from *their* childhood home?

Teach yourself to use your sense of humor. It can be a fantastic tool in tense moments.

It's nice to narrate stories from our childhood, even without any specific educational objectives. We can even tell about mistakes and errors we made, and how we overcame them.

Toddlers love to play with kitchenware. Let us allow them to do so.

Here's a fun game to play with the children: Everyone closes their eyes and walks around the room, shaking hands with the first person they encounter. Then the children must guess whose hand they shook.

An interesting question to ask the children: "If you could choose to be alone in the house with one of your siblings, whom would you choose? What would you want to do together with him or her?

Another interesting question to

pose to each child: "What is your favorite object in the house?"

Sit quietly in the room with your children and let them do their own thing. Pretend that you're watching an original children's play. You'll surely enjoy yourself and also learn something.

It is a good idea to disconnect the telephone when the children are eating together.

Encourage your children to involve Abba in their lives: to show him a picture they drew or an arts and crafts project they made, to tell him about a good grade in school, an activity they shared with their friends, and more.

Let your children help you cook: have them mix, taste, and even hand down their expert opinions of the results.

Try to figure out what are the most common words that are voiced within the four walls of your home.

Surprise your children with riddles. Tell jokes occasionally, and make an effort to "refresh" your supply.

Children will be happy to play their familiar nursery school and kindergarten games at home as well, such as *Duck, Duck, Goose*, *Red Light, Green Light*, and "*Mother, May I?*"

Next to family pictures in our album, we can record the cute things our children said at the time the picture was taken. (Be sure to label each picture with the date and place it was taken.)

Your daughter and her friends chose your house in which to get together and study for their test? Make it more pleasant for them by serving interesting refreshments.

Instead of going out on a vacation day, you can buy a new game, study the rules together with the children, and play with them. New games will entertain them for a long time, and the pleasure of being "together at home" is incomparable.

Are you planning on buying a new piece of furniture or household tool? You can ask the children for their opinions and even involve them in the shopping experience.

How lovely it is that in our family we consider each person individually—as well as everyone as a unit.

Count together with your children the coins that have accumulated in your tzedakah box, before you send off the money.

Collect interesting outfits and accessories in a box, and offer it to your children for imaginative games as well as plays. Watch these plays carefully and you will discover your children's hidden wishes and desires.

Together with your children, actively figure out tactics for the family to use to release tension. Then, when you find that tension is rising in the family, put the tactic to use: ring a special bell set aside for this purpose, count to ten, repeat a certain slogan, etc.

When you look in on your sleeping children, stroke their heads and whisper a *tefillah* over each child, from the depths of your heart. Your children will sense your love and dedication even when they are fast asleep.

Let us proclaim the following words in our home: "I forgive."

You'll be amazed at how pleasant it is to sit with the children opposite a tall pile of clean laundry as the older ones fold and the younger ones separate the folded clothes into piles for each person. You'll be surprised to learn that the little ones know which articles of clothing belong to which family member!

It is important to habituate family members to take the following statements seriously: "Chazal say…," "Tzaddikim used to …," "Bubby and

Zaidy used to say…"

Let us be gracious to people who arrive at our doorstep to collect food for the needy. And give your children the opportunity to hand over the contribution.

The long summer vacation days can be a wonderful opportunity to tackle some household projects together with your children. And what about a joint baking project with one child, or with all the children together?

When Bubby and Zaidy come, this is the time to say, "Bubby and Zaidy, look at your wonderful grandchildren!" Statements such as these will make all three generations feel happy.

To promote sibling harmony even from a very young age, hold the hand of the baby to stroke the faces of his brothers and sisters.

Do the children know Bubby's phone number by heart? If not, mark her phone number in the phone book with a colorful sticker.

Invest some serious, honest thought in figuring out which of our own behaviors tend to elicit unwelcome reactions from our children, and then avoid these. For instance, what reprimands of ours miss their mark, which tone of voice arouses tension, and what actions or punishments engender unwelcome responses.

Set aside a small closet or drawer for favorite books and games to be used only on Shabbos. This can be the "*oneg Shabbos* corner" in the children's room.

The home is a place where the whole group rejoices in the happiness of the individual, and where the pain of the individual is everyone's pain. It is in the home where concern and involvement toward others take root and grow.

Suggest to your son that he organize the *sefarim* together with his father as an enjoyable "togetherness activity."

Be sure to set aside a serving of your delicious meal for the brother who comes home late from yeshiva.

Hashem does so many kindnesses for us, day by day and hour by hour. In moments of gratitude, let us state our feelings to Hashem out loud in front of our children so that *Shem Shamayim* should be a familiar word on their tongues and in their hearts.

Let us emphasize the importance of *shalom* (peace) among all members of the family by mottos such as, "*Shalom* is important to all of

us," or "In our family, we are all willing to make an effort for *shalom*."

Let us be an example to our children of forgiveness and conciliation. Let us overlook minor differences of opinion and turn a blind eye to residues of anger and resentment, and instead focus our attention on those things that unify us and bring us together.

An important statement that we should make, when necessary, even in front of the children is, "We need to ask a *she'eilah*."

Amusing rhymes can help release tension during the "bewitching hour": "The food is ready, come to the table / The eggs are getting cold, this is no fable."

Hold your baby in your arms next to the flickering Shabbos candles and say, "Shabbat Shalom" out loud, with feeling and warmth.

The human mind resembles a tape that records images, sounds, tastes, and smells. It records continuously, then processes and stores records in our "memory box." Life events summon certain records to the threshold of the memory, and we retrieve them to use for our benefit. What records are recorded in the memory boxes of our children?

Not everything is absolute and definite in life. Sometimes we must use the words "perhaps," "it could be," "evidently." Sometimes there is room for a response such as, "I can't give you an answer right away; I have to consider it," or "I will think about it and give you an answer tomorrow."

You can invite cooperation by asking the question, "Who volunteers to do…?"

During tense moments, try to say the following in a calm, even voice: "Take a deep breath and count to ten," or "It will be more fun if we play by the rules." These kinds of statements often help break up a tense family atmosphere.

Let us utilize relaxed, free moments to impart educational messages to our children. Then, during confrontations and conflicts, we will only have to remind them of the lessons they have already learned.

Water is refreshing and cooling on hot summer days. Let your children play in water—perhaps they can even help with water-related cleaning activities such as hosing down the porch or washing the windows.

Every now and then, stop and check what our children have internalized at home as being important, and what they have internalized as being trivial or secondary.

It's a good idea to ask questions—to get the facts—before you arrive at conclusions.

Even a few well-chosen words can intensify familial feelings of love and brotherhood: "I'm happy to give it to you," "I enjoy doing this for you."

Observe your relaxed, satiated infant resting in your arms with a contented smile on his face, "like a suckling upon its mother" (*Tehillim* 131:2). You can learn *bitachon* in Hashem from him!

Understanding what we are saying intensifies *kavanah*, not only among older children but among younger children as well. Let us endeavor to explain a short paragraph each time to our children, according to their level of comprehension. Even small children are capable of understanding sections of the prayers and *birkas ha-mazon*.

You will truly *shep nachas* when you hear your children saying the following to each other: "What do you need now?" "How can I help you?" These statements express trust, kinship, and strength of the family bond.

How wonderful it is to belong to a home where family members say, "How can I help you?" or "Don't work so hard, let me lend you a hand." It's difficult to belong to a home where family members say, "Leave me alone, that's your problem."

Among statements heard in the home, we should add the following: "Sometimes we give to others, sometimes we take from others," "Sometimes we help others, sometimes we need to be helped," "Sometimes we can and sometimes we can't," "We are big and small at one and the same time," and "We have some things, and don't have others."

"Big" and "small" are relative terms; every single person is both "big" and "small" at one and the same time. We are "small" in that we are subordinate to *gedolei Torah* and *morei hora'ah*. We are "big" in that we are required to be responsible for ourselves and our actions, and sometimes we are also responsible for those younger than us.

It's impossible to understand everything, but as we get older and smarter we understand more. To illustrate this point to a seven-year-old, show him a math problem that's geared to a nine-year-old. He'll probably say, "But I'm only in second grade, and these kind of math problems are for fourth-graders!" Take advantage

of this opportunity to prove to him that ability and understanding develop with age and life experience.

Sometimes we need to say, "I don't know."

When a child comes to you with a problem, try to pose the following question in the plural: "What can we do to solve the problem?" Sometimes, the child with the problem also has the solution.

Involve your son who is learning in yeshiva with household doings when talking to him on the phone. Let him know that the baby has started to walk, or that you finally found someone to fix the squeaky door to the closet in his room.

Accustom yourself to making a *berachah* out loud on a piece of food or a drink before you feed the baby. The infant will learn from day one that no one puts anything in his mouth before making a *berachah*.

In honor of Shabbos, try occasionally to give small gifts to the children such as balloons, rings, or pictures. You might want to offer a selection of small items and let each child choose.

Instead of stating things as a complaint, turn them into polite requests. Instead of saying, "Why doesn't anyone in this house clear off the table?" say, "Please clear off the table."

Tell your children about the games you played when you were a child. Teach them these "old-fashioned" games and play with them.

Use proverbs from Tanach and Chazal to transmit messages, such as, "A tzaddik may fall seven times, but arises [each time again]" (*Mishlei* 24:16), "The faults a person finds in others are usually his own" (*Kiddushin* 70a), "Who is rich? He who is happy with what he has" (*Pirkei Avos* 4:1).

When the older children who go to an out-of-town yeshiva or seminary come home for vacation, let each of the smaller children have their own turn enjoying the company of their older brother or sister. Suggest that the younger ones prepare a small surprise for the "homecoming" such as a story, performance, or small homemade gift.

The written word can help express emotions and thoughts among family members. Save the various notes and letters in a special family album to preserve and perpetuate words that we all want to remember.

There are unavoidable days in every home when the atmosphere at home is bleak and gloomy, and even the children feel the tension in the air. It almost seems as if something is sucking everyone into a bad mood like a magnet. Take some time out to try to identify the cause of this negative atmosphere, so that you can take proactive steps to overcome its influence.

You and your children can say a chapter of *Tehillim* together for the recovery of sick Jews, or in praise of Hashem.

Your child is annoying and "nudgy"? Imagine that he is a guest or a neighbor's son. This will moderate our reaction; after all, we don't raise our voices to a child who is not our own.

Our messages and teachings are absorbed differently from child to child.

5

Rules, Regulations, and Limits

The Importance of Limits

Children need limits. They also need love, and appropriate limits serve to preserve that love. The nature of the home environment is to supply a child's needs with love and warmth. However, the home must also impose clear boundaries that delineate the child's sphere of activities, and ensure that the love will endure.

Limits or boundaries are the buffers between what is forbidden and what is permitted, between the possible and the impossible. They are very important for the proper development of the child. Setting rules and limits smoothes out the child's path and defines it, helping the child overcome his weaknesses and thus giving him the stability and confidence he needs. True, there are stages in a child's life where he will have difficulty accepting discipline and will even try to rebel because he wants immediate gratification without responsibilities. In fact, it may seem as if accepting regulations and limits goes against the child's real nature. But even then, a child will do best with limits that are imposed with a loving hand and educational forethought.

Moreover, in a home where rules and limits are consistently enforced, parents will be role models for their children, particularly for adolescents who yearn for maturity and independence. This is an opportunity to convince them that being an adult means standing firm and upholding the things you believe in.

No-Man's-Land

Erected along the border between two countries is a wall or barbed wire fence, as well as prominent signs that warn, "Stop! Border Ahead." If the border is not clearly defined or rigorously enforced, there may be attempts (by one country or the other) to penetrate into the no-man's-land between the forbidden and the permitted. (Between hostile countries, wars of attrition are held as one or both sides attempt to cross the lines.) This is analogous to the situation in most homes. While some issues are clear in the family and no one dares to cross the line, other issues are less clear-cut and more "fuzzy" because the parents are less decisive about them.

How are fuzzy lines drawn in homes? If we observe closely, we will discover that when parents set clear boundaries and define them for their children, then the children generally accept them and do not raise objections. But when the parents themselves are unsure about the limits or do not make them sufficiently clear to their children, then the children are more likely to test these limits.

Testing the Limits

When a parent is not decisive enough, or when a child does not really understand her parent's message, the child may attempt to test the limits. If she is successful, she will conclude that limits or borders may, in fact, be shifted. This child is likely to spend most of her time planted firmly in the narrow "demilitarized zone" beside the border, while investing most of her efforts in trying to move it. Examples of "border times" may be when Ima is talking on the phone or to a neighbor who has stopped by. During this time, the border seems less firm and durable than usual. Perhaps this is the time to sneak a forbidden cookie, for example. Consequently, the child is occupied with the wall and neglects to spread out and take advantage of the entire expanse of permitted living space open to her.

Unstable, shifting limits actually interfere with the child's ability to enjoy the full spectrum of permitted activities because a child who invests all her efforts in obtaining a forbidden cookie will not be able to enjoy the chocolate bar she is given instead. When the limits and frameworks are not clear, children spend much effort on achieving what is forbidden and in attempting to move the boundaries. Only clear boundaries and limits create a calm, relaxed living space.

Setting New Routines within the Family Framework

Let us take the example of changing the clock to daylight savings time. This change necessitates adaptation of the entire family to a change in daylight hours and engenders difficulty in putting children to sleep while it is still light out.

As parents who lead and are not led, we must decide in advance what are the most appropriate bedtime hours for the new season that most of the family can deal with. Of course, we must take into account all the household members when we institute the new rou-

tine, and should also occasionally check to make sure it fits in with the new realities.

Call a family meeting to discuss the changes entailed by moving the clock. Listen to what the children think and make sure they understand what we really mean by "moving the clock," then bring up the problem: the regular bedtime hours will now fall when it is still light outside. What should we do?

Let the children express what they think; a child who is a partner to decisions will be more likely to implement them willingly. Of course, this is true only for those parts of a decision in which we can involve the children and take their opinions into account. For example, we might consider their suggestion to hang heavy curtains in their bedroom to block out the sun, but reject their request to move their bedtime ahead a full hour later.

The next stage is to set the rule: what will be the new bedtime hours for the younger family members as well as for the slightly older ones, and the date for the commencement of the new rule, such as "in two weeks."

Talk about rules as family conventions or norms, not as requests that serve our personal interests. You could say, "In our home, we eat supper at seven o'clock," instead of, "Ima wants you to be ready to eat at seven." The rule should not become a bone of contention between "them" and "us," and should fall on all household members equally but with appropriate modifications as necessary. For instance, teenagers might not need a new bedtime when the clocks change, but perhaps their curfew can be extended an hour during daylight savings time.

Don't end the family meeting until you check that each child understands the practical implications of the decision on him or her (such as changes in the time frame for homework or showers). Each child should accept responsibility for carrying out the new rule and be aware of the rewards and consequences involved—which should have some logical connection to the act. For example, a child who doesn't get to bed on time might have to go to bed that much earlier the next night.

Parents should assist in helping the children become accustomed to the new routine. Perhaps for the first two weeks of the new rule, parents should not invite guests at this hour or answer the phone. Thus the children learn that their parents are serious about and consistent with their decisions, making sure that they are carried out.

"Supportive compensation" can do wonders during this adjustment period. Thus when bedtimes go back an hour due to changing the clocks back to standard time, parents can tell a special bedtime story or play a new tape to ease the process.

Administer reminders clearly, succinctly, and in an authoritative tone of voice. Remind the children occasionally what the consequences of disobedience are, but try to radiate trust in and not doubt of the children's ability to carry out the new rules.

Non-adherence to rules should be treated with the (unpleasant) "natural consequences" that stem from the violation itself. For example, a child who eats a forbidden chocolate before dinner should not be given the dessert enjoyed by the rest of the family after dinner. This will reinforce the parents' goals and give them greater weight. In general, obedience to parents should be created by firm but courteous parental authority, not by aggressive displays of power. Parents should demonstrate self-control, understanding, and consideration as well as flexibility. They should carefully consider their children's needs and opinions before setting new rules.

However, not every rule needs an explanation. Household members should also obey such statements as, "We do this because Abba and

Ima decided that this is best for the family," or even, "Because I said so." Just as in the Torah there are *chukim*, for which no explanation is given, alongside *mishpatim*, for which reasons are given, so, too, not everything in the home needs persuasion or explanation. Just as we accept *chukim* in Judaism, we can accept that Abba's and Ima's rules are also "family *chukim*" which we follow even when we don't understand them.

In every home there are rules that set limits and preserve love. How do we determine the rules in our home? What gives them their strength and stability? How can we continue to place limits as needed for the benefit of the entire family? Following are points to consider.

A child views his parents as leaders who know how to set limits when needed.

When you forbid something to your children, adopt a decisive and authoritative tone of voice. Tape yourself and listen to yourself speak so that you can modify your tone of voice if necessary.

It is important to transmit the following message in your home: In every house there is a parent(s) who decides what is right for their children.

When you have to rebuke or criticize your child, try to formulate what you say in general terms rather than as direct accusations, such as, "Jumping from high steps causes falls, and children can hurt themselves this way."

When your child heads off to her first day in pre-school, make it a little easier for her by allowing her to take a favorite doll or object with her from home.

How pleasant it is when a child has good telephone manners! Teach your children how to answer the phone courteously, and even to offer to take messages.

When there is a difference of opinion, it is all right to say,

"Now we are the parents and you are the children. When you will be parents, your children will have to listen to you."

When you hear noise from the children's room during rest time, you can say, "You seem to have forgotten that Abba is sleeping now. I'm sure you will keep quiet from now on."

A timer is a valuable tool that can be put to good use throughout the day. For example, you can play "Beat the Clock," saying, "Let's see who will be ready for bed when the timer rings!"

Your six-year-old daughter "must" play with her dolls when she comes home from school, while you feel she should do her homework immediately. Examine what is "*al pi darko*" for your daughter in order to decide what is an acceptable request to make of her. For example, perhaps she is the type who needs "down time" before she sits down to do more schoolwork, but will willingly do it after she has eaten and rested.

Before setting limits for your children, decide in your own mind what is the absolute limit and on what issues you are willing to compromise. This will narrow the range of possible objections of family members.

Children absorb educational messages mainly from personal example, and less from lectures.

Sometimes, you can release a child from his usual chores around the house. After all, everyone deserves an occasional vacation.

If you decide that you will allow your child to have a candy later and not right now, try to show him or her that you are putting the candy away in a "safe place" for later on.

When you want your children to do something, you will find that giving them a choice serves to lessen their resistance. For example, you can say, "Would you prefer to clean up your room before dinner or after?" or "Do you prefer to wash the dishes or clear off the table?"

Sometimes, the best explanation is, "We do this because Abba and Ima say so."

Honor your children's "private domains." When your daughter closets herself in her room with her friends, respect their privacy.

When we buy new shoes, we allow our feet time to get used to them. We must also give ourselves time to adjust to new habits or rules in the home. Let us remember this, and remain patient.

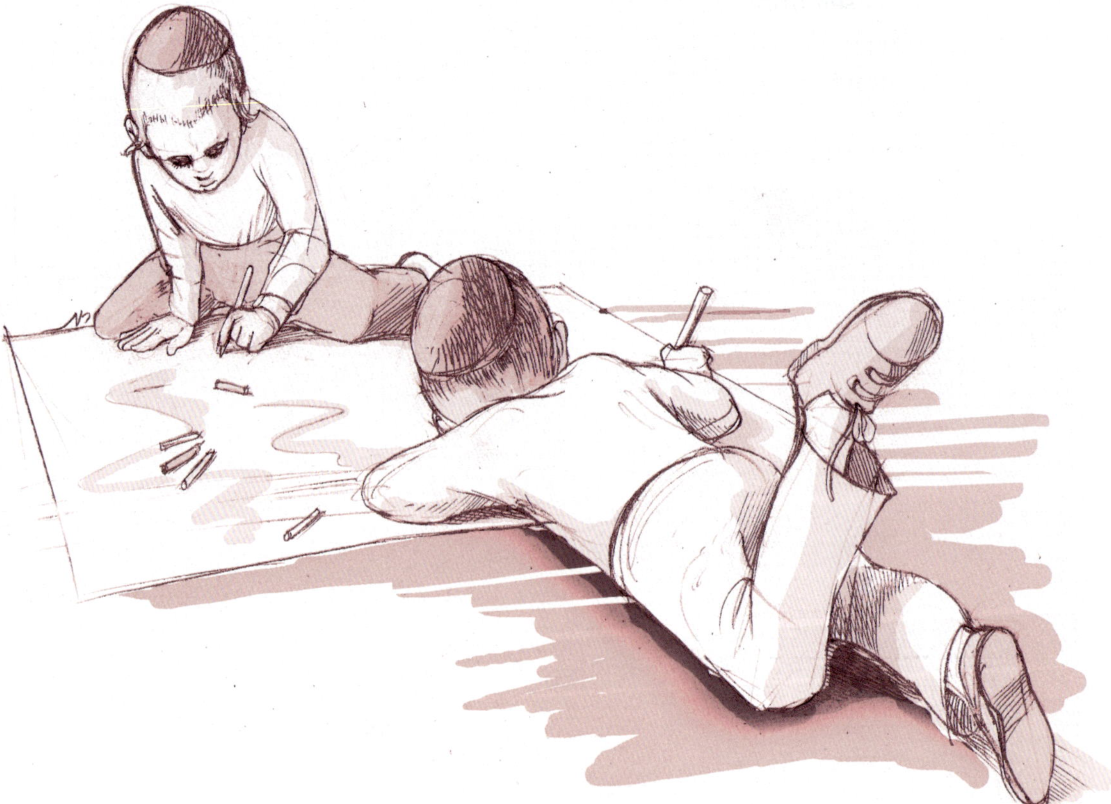

When a situation or request catches you by surprise and you find yourself unprepared, answer without committing yourself by saying, "This is the first time I've seen/heard this. I must think what is the proper thing to do." This will save you from rash decisions and regret.

Sometimes the best response in a situation is to take action, without saying a word.

While family procedures and timetables must be clear, a wise parent knows how to be flexible when a child wants to do things a little differently from everyone else, "*al pi darko*." For example, some children like to draw pictures when stretched out on the floor, instead of at a table. Try to allow them to do this, whenever possible.

When delegating authority in the house, you can assign the older children partial responsibility over the younger ones, such as putting them in charge of dressing them or feeding them supper.

Try to take notice of even minor positive changes in your children's behavior. Even slight progress can be significant.

Teenage girls feel that they "MUST" talk at length to their friends on the telephone. However, parents MUST set clear limits on these phone conversations so the home can function properly. Of course, parents MUST also be flexible.

The clock is a neutral "discipline catalyst." You can employ it to display an agreed-upon time to limit as well as delineate certain activities. Set it in a central place in the house so you can use it to demonstrate time-related concepts.

When routine chores become tiresome, switch them among the family members to refresh everyone's energies.

When it's time to put the children to sleep, put aside all your other activities and focus on making sure that the family procedures are carried out systematically—brushing teeth, washing up, and so forth.

It's a good idea to inform the children in advance of the probable result of their actions. For example, you can say, "If you go to sleep early, you will be able to get up early the next morning."

A parent who sets clear boundaries allows his child to use the available space within the limits.

Sudden braking is bad on the car and causes it to shake. Drastic "braking" of unwelcome behavior among children can also cause shock.

Instead, wait patiently until the children's "motor" turns off on its own. For example, if your eight-year-old son starts drinking chocolate milk ten minutes before dinner, he might not put the glass down immediately when you tell him to stop. He might "need" to take one or two more sips before he can "turn off" this behavior and go on to the next.

Silence is golden; and sometimes sitting and doing nothing—*shev v'al ta'aseh*—is the most appropriate action of them all.

Children learn in zigzags: "Two steps forward, one step back." Even when you think there hasn't been any progress, take a look back; you may see that there has been movement from the starting point!

An authoritative statement such as, "Abba decided," should be accepted unequivocally.

To achieve order, we often must first endure a period of disorder and upheaval—an experience we all undergo every year during our hectic Pesach preparations before the well-organized Seder. We should apply this principle to the realm of childrearing as well, and gird ourselves with patience instead of giving in to despair.

Be prepared to hear and accept complaints and dissatisfaction

from your children when they object to some of your rules. But this is no reason to abolish appropriate regulations and limits.

When a child fails, he or she will find it difficult to answer your question of, "Why?" Instead, ask, "What can be done now to correct the situation?" Often, this will lead to cooperation as well as creative ideas for solutions.

Fixed habits and routines in the daily schedule impart confidence and inner calmness, as the child knows exactly what to expect.

Younger children tend to accept parental rulings as-is, while older children prefer to be consulted before decisions are made concerning them.

Children seek freedom and enjoyment, while parents educate them toward delayed gratification, restraint, and self-control.

When helping your young child prepare for bedtime, you can state the necessary actions out loud: "Now we take off our shoes...we get into bed, we say *Shema*," and so forth.

Try to act as an advocate for your child, even as you insist that he or she act appropriately. For example you can say, "I know that you were tired and tense, but despite that I still expect you to avoid shouting at your sister the way you did yesterday."

"The workers are lazy...and the master is insistent" (*Pirkei Avos* 3:20)—Nevertheless, we should still try to be patient and tolerant as we prod our children!

As parents, we also sometimes stumble and fall. If we can identify the petty and childish element that hides in us and emerges precisely during moments of weakness, it will help us overcome this "inner enemy."

A statement such as, "You need to be in bed at seven o'clock, but it's up to you whether bedtime will be pleasant or not," gives the child the opportunity to accept the routine and take responsibility for his or her choices.

The baby needs to go to sleep now. But the family is having such a great time playing with him. What will we choose to do?

Train your children to keep a special list on which they record those items they loan to others and those that others lend them.

Sometimes it is best to turn a blind eye to an annoying but temporary occurrence, such as a group of mischievous

children running noisily through the house.

Babies will extend their hands time after time to obtain an out-of-reach toy, never giving up. What a wonderful example for us of persistence and determination!

When a child shows restraint and control, let us remember to respond out loud; for example, "You wanted to take but decided to give; you are growing up!"

It's pleasant to hear encouraging words even for chores that have long become part of one's daily routine, such as, "I always enjoy seeing the neat beds you make in the morning!"

6 Feeling Our Feelings

IT IS AN ORDINARY morning. The telephone rings, and you hear your mother-in-law's voice on the line. "You are such a gracious hostess and so good at planning affairs," she gushes, "I just knew you'd be delighted to prepare one of the Sheva Berachos for our new kallah, right?" You try to say something, but your mother-in-law doesn't let you get a word in edgewise. "You've proved yourself so many times, you don't have to say a word—I rely on you a hundred percent."

That's it, the conversation is over and you don't know what to do with yourself! You call a good friend and pour out your heart to her. "You'll never believe what just happened on the phone!" You tell her the whole story, and how your mother-in-law's request—more like a command—overwhelmed you. "Of course I'd like to help out, but I really don't see how I can take on such a project now." You narrate the facts to your friend, but you also express emotions. What you expect from your friend? Do you really want advice now, or to be told what to do? Do you want someone to give you *mussar* and tell you that you should be delighted to prepare a Sheva Brachos, and that you're blowing this out of proportion?

Or perhaps you only seek a sympathetic ear and an understanding heart...

Emotional Outpouring

During periods of "emotional outpouring," most people want others to listen to them, understand, and sympathize. They hope to hear words that express empathy such as, "To impose such a big project like that on you, without even asking you if you agree!" Emotional outpouring is like detergent that foams up in a basin. The bubbles cover the water so that you can only see the water after the bubbles dissolve. Similarly, people need to calm down via emotional empathy so that their logic can take over and they can find solutions.

The Difference between Adults and Children

Children need empathy even more than adults, because children speak the language of emotion. When a child says, "I want to hit you," he is expressing anger. When he asks us to please give the new baby away to Bubby as a gift, he probably is experiencing a sense of deprivation or discrimination. A child who complains about the bad weather that caused the cancellation of a long-awaited trip feels disappointment. When he says, "My teacher is great," he may be happy over the good grade he received on a recent test.

An adult is accustomed to dealing logically with the facts of life and responding realistically to changing circumstances. The child, on the other hand, responds via his or her emotions. Our job as adults and parents is to decipher the emotions that fuel a child's words or even actions, and help him or her cope with them. Unfortunately our tendency is to relate only to the facts because as adults, we are more connected to facts than emotions. However, as parents and educators it is important that we connect emotionally to our children. In order to do this, *we must uncover our own natural emotional capabilities*.

We must remember that our children are still on the "first floor" while we, the adults, are on the second. The "children's floor" contains emotions and instincts while our floor contains insight and control. The principle of teaching a child *al pi darko*, according to his nature, requires us to descend to the child on his level, and gradually help him grow from there.

"My best friend is moving to another neighborhood, and she won't be my best friend anymore," your daughter laments. Her statement expresses a number of feelings: loneliness, apprehension, and longing for her friend. How can we help her? We must identify the emotions behind her words and respond in such a way that shows that we understand her: "You're afraid that when your friend moves you will feel lonely," "Even now you miss her, and that makes it hard for you."

Our response to the child's emotions helps the child recognize his own emotions, express them, then cope with them. Just as a child becomes familiar with the "bodily me" in the mirror, he learns to recognize his "emotional me" by hearing us adults reflect his emotions.

Our ultimate goal is to educate the child, and emotional connection is a bridge to this. You cannot educate a child who is overwhelmed with emotions, just as you can't give swimming lessons to a drowning person. To demonstrate this principle, let's take the case of a mother holding her infant in her arms while her three-year-old son persistently bothers her and the baby. What is the emotion behind the unwelcome actions? Perhaps the three-year-old feels deprivation or jealousy. When the child experiences an emotion he immediately puts it into action, and that is why he hits and scratches now.

The automatic response of the worried mother is to try to "educate" the child, saying, "It's not nice to hit a little baby!" Instead, try to identify the emotion at work here—the need of the child to feel confident in his mother's love—and satisfy that emotion by exhibiting your motherly love to the three-year-old with hugs and attention. This will calm him down more than reprimands and lectures. The sensitive and considerate atmosphere you create will plant confidence, trust and openness in the child, enabling him to accept his mother's guidance.

Four Steps toward the Goal

There are four steps to achieving an emotional connection: listening, identifying the feeling that hides under the verbiage, assigning a name to this feeling, and inserting it into our conversation. The emotional connection created via these steps will replace a child's stormy emotions. Moreover, only after going through all four stages is the child ready to use her own logic to try to solve the problem. It is interesting to note that in most cases, the child herself makes the transfer to using logic without assistance from her parents. However, it is important that we plant ourselves firmly at her side during her moments of coping with stormy emotions. By offering her our shoulder to lean on, the child's emotional outpouring tends to subside and she becomes ready to listen to the voice of reason.

Meivin u'Ma'azin, Mabit u'Makshiv

How do we listen? First of all, we must set aside all other tasks that distract us. We cannot really listen when we are reading the newspaper or frying an omelet. We must concentrate when we listen, and make sure that our "active listening" includes all four necessary components: understand, give ear to, look, and pay attention.

***Meivin*/Understand**—to listen correctly means that you want to understand the other before being understood in turn, which is the opposite of our normal human inclination.

***Ma'azin*/Give ear to**—literally, but in a way that you express interest and concentration.

***Mabit*/Look**—try to maintain eye contact and remain face-to-face.

***Makshiv*/Pay attention**—listen with a real desire to hear and respond with such "listening" sounds as, "uh huh," "oy vey," "hmm...," "I understand."

Let's take the case of nine-year-old Tamar who is sent by her mother to the local grocery store to buy a carton of milk. When she finally returns, she has empty hands and a worried look on her face. It turns out, from the half-sentences she emits, that on her way home from the store she stopped to play with her friends and doesn't remember where she left the milk. Tamar's mother listens, identifies and gives name to her daughter's emotions, and connects with them. First she responds without words, with a face expressing empathy. Perhaps she will also put a hand on Tamar's shoulder. Then she calms down her daughter and says, "How sorry you were when you realized that you'd lost the milk!" This kind of response creates a bridge between mother and daughter. The daughter feels that she is understood, her pain lessens, and her love for her mother becomes stronger because "Ima understands me."

Tamar can now be sent to look for the lost milk container. Perhaps she will return with empty hands; maybe she will even burst into tears. But it is very likely that afterwards, Tamar will come to the decision to be much more careful in the future, and it is not even necessary that her mother tell her this outright. The "I am with you in your trouble" attitude from the mother will give Tamar the momentum she needs to acquire responsibility. It will also instill in her a deep feeling of emotional confidence because she is understood.

It is clear that during the listening and identification stage, we hold ourselves back from "detective" questions such as, "On what street did you play with your friends?" or "Did you see anyone walk off with the milk?" and certainly avoid accusations such as, "This isn't the first time that you acted irresponsibly and disappointed me!" These kinds of responses are likely to sever emotional connections, not foster them.

Do not attempt to give advice during times of trouble. A child who suffers a humiliating failure or other unpleasant experience doesn't need an adult to smother him immediately with premature tips and advice. This is similar to the case of a child whose glasses fall and break, and in order to help him his parent gives him the parent's own glasses. Clearly, good intentions notwithstanding, this is not appropriate assistance. It is not enough to teach your child; you must be able to listen to and empathize with him.

The Language of Feeling—Pinpointing Emotions and Expressing Them Verbally

In order to develop awareness of our emotional world, we must first develop the language of feeling and learn to recognize the many expressions we, and our families, have for emotions. For example, a child may come home from school after failing a test and say, "I am so very angry," when he really is disappointed. It is important that we gently explain to him the exact name for his feelings—in this case, disappointment instead of anger. Another example is the child who says, "I'm scared about my test tomorrow," when he really is worried.

We should teach our children to distinguish between feelings such as worry, sadness, embarrassment, insult, loneliness, longing, excitement, calm, mercy, compassion, pleasantness, satisfaction, enjoyment, warmth, love, and more. By enriching the child's emotional vocabulary, we help him pinpoint the appropriate feeling and help him deal with it in an appropriate manner. One practical way of doing this is to sit with our children, talk about real-life experiences with them, and then discuss and describe the emotions we experienced. We can also do this when reading stories aloud to them by identifying the feelings of the protagonists. We can also use drama and plays.

The Fear of Reinforcing Unwelcome Emotions

We can divide up the gamut of human emotions into four branches: fear, sadness, anger, and pleasure. If we track our responses to our child, we will see that when our child comes to tell us about a successful experience we feel happiness and satisfaction and our natural reaction is to express our positive feelings while connecting emotionally. "That's wonderful!" we'll say, or "That makes Ima so happy!" Usually, we'll wait with our "detective" questions until a later stage, such as clarifying the details of the successful experience and the exact events connected to it.

But what happens when the child expresses fear, sadness, or anger—emotions we perceive as difficult and undesirable? In these cases, we shy away from connecting to these feelings because we are afraid of reinforcing them. For example, when children express fear we feel that we must protect them. We worry that if we connect emotionally to the frightened child, the child will conclude that his or her fear is justified and thus we will have intensified the fears. In order to prevent this, we try to bring the voice of logic into our response. When our child says, "I'm scared to sleep in the dark," we try to abolish this fear and prove that there is no rational reason to fear. But a child who is emotionally flooded is simply not capable of using logic at this moment. "When it's dark in my room, I see bears walking on the wall!" our son cries in increasing agitation. What can you as a mother do to help him? First of all, connect emotionally, as in the dialogue below:

Ima: *Oy, you see bears on the wall. That can be very scary…*

Child: *Yes, I am very frightened. See, they are looking straight at me.*

Ima: *Tell me how many bears you see.*

Child: *I think…maybe….*

Ima: *Which one frightens you the most?*

Child: *The big bear!*

You will notice that if you continue the discussion for another few sentences, the child's attack of fright will start to abate, and not intensify, as a result of the conversation.

The next day, you might want to suggest drawing the bears with your son and ask what he thinks the two of you should do to them. The child might offer his own suggestions for overcoming fear. The mother's emotional connection soothes the child, helps him free himself from the fear, and advances him toward listening to the voice of reason.

A similar scenario takes place when our son or daughter expresses pain and sadness and we are too quick to comfort the child. Again, we tend to avoid connecting emotionally with the feelings of pain and sadness so as not to reinforce them. We rush to offer solutions to relieve the suffering and pain.

But the sad child needs us to connect to his feelings, and needs our empathy when he is deep in his sadness. Only after he feels that we are with him can he strengthen himself and calm down to receive our suggestions. Sometimes he finds his own means to comfort himself.

The following example will demonstrate the principles involved:

Your daughter had to part from a dear friend who moved far away. She is depressed and anguished. In the midst of her pain, don't try to offer solutions. Listen to her intently while you sit close by, perhaps even hug and stroke her. Respond with such comments as, "It's so sad to say good-bye," "It's hard for you to go on without your friend," "You feel so empty inside; your heart cries all the time." Only after a time-out period, when we see that the channels of communication and understanding are opening, can we gradually attempt to transmit a message of encouragement. It's important to remember that emotional connection in and of itself encourages and strengthens, and giving a child time to process her pain, while we support her, strengthens and prepares her for life's disappointments.

And how do we respond when a child expresses anger? Again, we view anger as a negative emotion and feel a need to teach the child and immediately halt the anger. Shmulik comes home from cheder and shouts angrily, "I wish Chananya weren't in my class!" Often, a mother recoils from connecting emotionally with such unseemly thoughts so as not to seem to legitimize negative behavior.

How, then, should you respond? Perhaps you're tempted to gesture to your child that you don't want to hear his harsh words, that he's crossed the line with his behavior. But wait: yes, you want your child to watch what he says and how he says it, but on the other hand—you don't want to stop him from bringing his distress home. You want him to continue bringing his experiences, even negative ones, home, because it is in the home that children receive the strength to overcome and cope. During times like these, it would be wise to overlook the child's angry outpourings. You might want to use responses such as, "I see you've had a very hard day today," "Ouch, that hurts," "It's hard for you when Chananya does X." These responses link you to the child's distress and facilitate an emotional connection that will be the fertile ground for receptiveness to parental guidance in the future. Remember: we cannot expect a child who is in an emotional state to be available for logical analysis and direction. As we learn from Chazal (*Pirkei Avos* 4:17), "Do not try to appease your fellowman when he is angry."

Parents are afraid that if they spend too much time with their child dwelling on emotional experiences that are painful, disturbing or frightening, the situation is likely to become permanent, and they will never be able to return to the world of reason and logic. This is the fear of reinforcing negative emotions. But this concern is false. Remember that if you do not make an emotional connection, your child's quandary will only deepen, he will lose trust in you, and then he might try to seek help for his troubles elsewhere—not necessarily in the right place or with the right people. Instead, choose your words carefully when your child expresses negative emotions and keep in mind an important rule: Understanding does not mean agreement; you can understand but not condone.

If your daughter comes home and says, "I'm not going to school anymore!" you can listen, nod your head, and even say, "I see that you're really upset." This response expresses understanding for your daughter's distress, but does not convey agreement that she can quit school. You understand, but are not attempting to offer solutions because you want to provide a time-out for her stormy emotions to subside. Only then will you be able to rise to the "second floor" for a logical solution, "*al pi darko*."

Emotional Connection as a Bridge to Constructive Communication

To summarize, emotional connection is the precursor to proper communication. It creates a bridge of trust between parents and children, a bridge that will later be used for transmitting educational lessons and emotional support. The emotional connection stage is the sincere, initial stage of "I am with him in time of trouble" (*Tehillim* 91:15).

If we don't allow a place for this important stage, our children are likely to distance themselves from us and cut off emotional contact, with the feeling that "no one understands me," "no one cares," "there is no one to talk to." When children are in emotional pain, we must be with them in their distress and allow them to experience these painful emotions at our side. Emotional identification with our children will enable them to cope better with their feelings and gain confidence before they proceed, together with us, to the realm of logic and problem-solving. Our support at this stage bestows on our children the strength to cope with the vicissitudes of life and a willingness to accept our parental guidance in the years to come.

Tasty Morsels

Food for thought: Consider for a moment how much our eyes are turned to Hashem and how all of our hopes and aspirations depend on Him. That is how our children feel about us, their parents, as they are dependent on us for all their needs.

"Something similar happened to me as well when I was a young girl; I also felt that way." A sentence like this will be accepted as an honest, open show of identification with our child.

Try to acquire "emotional sensors" to pick up the message beyond the words themselves. Before responding to what your child is saying, try to uncover the emotion and the meta-message hiding behind the words.

It is important to express empathy with your child's pain, in words. When your son is in distress, it is good for him to hear that you are with him and that you do not look down on him for his emotions.

When you sense that your daughter has been somewhat pushed off to the side or "lost in the shuffle," devote a bit of personal attention to her. Bring her a flower with a loving note and place it on her private bedroom shelf.

When there is a change in your child's routine—your son has a new rebbe or your daughter's seat in the classroom has been moved—don't forget to show your interest and inquire how he or she is coping with the change.

When a child comes home in pain, sometimes words are superfluous. Just hug him and offer him a treat.

When your child is happy, and you are trying to express to her how radiant she looks, take out a mirror and show her the lovely expression on her face.

When your youngest asks, "Who do you love the most out of all the children?" you are in a very awkward position. One way to deal with this is to say, "Out of all the Dovid'ls, Ima loves this Dovid'l the best; out of all the Rochel'es, Ima loves her Rochel'e the best!"

Find time to sit opposite each child individually and concentrate on listening to him or her. If one of them says, "I want to be little because everyone loves the little ones," he is telling you what bothers him. Encourage him to talk about it.

Our faces express what we feel inside. Ask one of the children to express an emotion on his

or her face, then have the others try to guess the emotion.

Your two-year-old disturbs his older brothers in order to "connect" to those closest to him. Teach him positive communication; perhaps give him a candy and say, "Do you want to be friendly with your brother? Give him the candy." Perhaps you can take his hand and use it to gently stroke his brothers' faces.

"Find a real friend." Let us guide our children toward investing in real friendships; understanding someone else's feelings, learning what they like and need, and sensing when they need company or when they want to be alone or with their family.

Food for thought: Consider what the child is likely to say to herself in response to what you say to her; and think about what you say to yourself in response to what she says to you.

Children love books about animals. Animal fables are wonderful tools for demonstrating emotions, traits, and behaviors—negative as well as positive.

Although most people like it when we show an interest in their lives and activities, there are some children who do not like others to pry into their personal matters. Let's try to avoid asking questions that our children don't like to answer.

When your children ask you to assume the role of judge among "warring factions," summarize the complaints of both sides with expressions of understanding, "Yes, it hurts when someone yanks a toy away from you just when you are playing with it." Then, express your faith in their abilities by saying, "Sit down together, the two of you, and think of a solution. I am prepared to help you." Hopefully, they will eventually reach a compromise and the argument will vanish.

When children complain about unwanted actions of their siblings or friends, you can say, "I'm not interested in what someone else did, but I am *very* interested in hearing about *you*! Tell me what you think and feel."

It is important to rejoice in the good news of others, and to express your joy in words.

Your daughter comes home from school angry; her classmates disturbed the teacher. Try to teach her that instead of criticizing others, she can think, "What should I do when this happens? How can I help to improve the situation?"

Sometimes a young child feels

bitter and angry that her sister is so relaxed and cheerful with her own friends, yet so impatient with her, the little sister. Consider whether she feels rejected by her sister; this may be the reason she starts up with her and causes arguments.

Some children like a "time-out" period when they come home from school; they want to be alone with themselves in their home. It is important to leave them alone for a while and postpone questions and requests until a later hour.

Get on the floor and give yourself the opportunity to become acquainted with your house from your baby's point of view.

It's important to remember that there is no such thing as a difficult child; rather, there is a child having difficulties.

Sit with your child and look at a family photo album or illustrated book. Try to label the emotions you see on people's faces, and point out less familiar emotions your child may not recognize.

Often, a child's automatic reaction to the question of "Why" is, "Because." If you really want an answer to a question, try to find a different way to phrase it.

Tears are a wonderful way to express and dissipate hurtful emotions. It is important to allow them and respect them at any age.

For children, emotions are operative orders. When they are hurt, they cry; when they are afraid, they shout; when they are happy, they clap their hands. As they mature, let us show them additional ways of expressing emotions as well as how to restrain themselves and postpone gratification.

A child who bothers others is usually a child who is troubled and feels so tangled up that he can't see a way out. Try to find some way to communicate with him and to guide him in finding his way out of the maze: "It seems to me that you would also like to participate in the game. Let's think together how you will be able to join the others."

Bedtime, when your children are relaxing peacefully in their beds, is a wonderful opportunity for heart-to-heart talks with them.

Let us gradually instruct our children to discriminate between thoughts and emotions: "You think you will be going on a trip, so you feel happy."

Encourage children to express their emotions through drawing, painting, or clay modeling.

We learn in *Sefer HaChinuch*, אחרי הפעולות נמשכים הלבבות—our actions eventually lead our hearts in the same direction. We can demonstrate this principle to our children by saying, “Yesterday when I was upset, I davened with great *kavanah* and afterwards I felt calm and secure.” Or we can tell our child, “I saw how you helped Bubby and Zaidy carry their suitcases into the house. I'm sure you felt really good about it.”

You enrich your children's emotional language when you describe your own emotions to them by saying things such as, “I was disappointed when…,” “It makes me happy when…”

Ask your children to guess how you feel when Sruli makes a *berachah* out loud, Michali forgot her lunch bag at home, Bubby asks you to take her to the doctor, the baby cries at night, Yanki learns with Abba.

7

Ma'achil u'Mashkeh— Serving Our Parents

Kibud horim, HONORING OUR parents, is one of the "rational" or intuitive mitzvos that we are commanded in our holy Torah. All human beings understand that it is incumbent upon them to honor the people who brought them into the world, raised them, and supported them until they were able to stand on their own. But what is the proper way to honor parents? We, the Jewish nation, are unique among all the nations of the world in that we honor our parents by virtue of a Godly commandment, and by Godly criterion.

Teaching *Kibud Horim* as a Mitzvah

The Torah tells us, "Honor your father and your mother" (*Shemos* 20:12). Rashi explains this in *Vayikra* 19:3: "What is *kavod*, honor?

It is *ma'achil u'mashkeh*—providing food and drink to our parents, providing them with clothing and shoes, leading them into and out of [a room]." Thus we learn that the essence of honoring our parents lies in physically doing for them such seemingly simple tasks as feeding and clothing them. Consequently, we must guide our children to this kind of giving from *gil ha-chinuch*, i.e., the earliest age they are able to perform this mitzvah.

In order to accomplish this, we must overcome psychological obstacles embedded in human nature: "A father has mercy on his son but his son does not have mercy on him [his father], only on his own son" (*Sotah* 49a). Parents possess unlimited desire to give their children as much as possible, while children do not feel this same need to benefit their parents. Rav Yechiel Meir from Ostrovtza explains this by saying that the devotion of a parent to his children is an innate, inherited trait from Adam HaRishon to his descendents. But the devotion of a child to his parents is not an inherited or inborn trait; it must be acquired and learned. Parents must educate their children toward *kibud horim*. To do so, they must control and restrain themselves from their natural tendency to give; the children, on the other hand, must habituate themselves to give, and not always to take.

Parents who educate their children in this way develop in the latter the emotional and intellectual ability to appreciate their obligations toward their parents as well as to proactively discern their parents' needs and fulfill them. Our sources attest to the fact that in past generations, many sons and daughters devoted themselves to almost limitless giving of themselves to their parents while in this generation, the situation has unfortunately declined; education has weakened in the home and we have become more selfish. We are witness to a different situation now; parents constantly rack their brains trying to figure out what to give their children that they haven't yet given them, while children keep on taking and taking without being taught how to acquire for themselves the ability to give.

Creating Conditions for Fulfilling the Commandment

In order to develop in our children the proper approach to the mitzvah of *kibud horim*, it is important to provide opportunities for them to recognize that their parents also have needs and that we, the parents, are prepared to accept help from our children in fulfilling these needs. For example, Ima comes home from work on a hot afternoon carrying a heavy shopping bag. Her seven-year-old daughter runs toward her, ready to tell about her day in school, while her three-year-old son points to a snack he sees peeking out of the shopping bag. But Ima is thirsty and her feet hurt. How wonderful it would be if one of the children would bring her a cup of cold water, or even bring her comfortable slippers! Clearly, children will not think of doing these things on their own; they must be directed. You, the mother, can learn to say pleasantly, "Who will please bring me something to drink? And who wants to bring me my slippers?" The children thus learn to fulfill their mother's needs before they turn to her with their own needs and requests.

Other scenarios: Abba comes home and politely instructs one of the children to take his hat and put it away. Or Ima is busy in the kitchen and asks one of the younger children to please bring her the cordless phone.

Some parents feel important and strong only when they give: "When I give, I am worthwhile." They feel that when they take from their children their worth is diminished and they are showing weakness. Such parents will find it easier to take from their children if they realize that this taking is, in fact, imparting to their children the joy and satisfaction of giving! When parents let their children help them, they provide the children with an important opportunity for feeling self-worth, and bequeath to their children the *zechus* for a mitzvah whose reward is long life—"... so that you may live longer" (*Shemos* 20:12).

Sometimes we are inhibited from this task by societal pressures, or even perceived societal pressures. We wonder to ourselves, what will my neighbors and friends think of me when they see me sitting down and resting while my children run errands for me? Won't that make me look like a selfish person who takes advantage of her children for her personal needs? In short, we are embarrassed to fly in the face of societal norms around us—norms which are not based on *da'as Torah* at all but usually on the "*da'as*" of society and individuals. What a pity to let erroneous "conventional wisdoms" prevent us from educating our children properly!

Kibud Horim—Mikarev Levavos

Even simple acts of giving, such as "to feed and to clothe" as mentioned in the halachah, affect the parent-child connection far beyond the narrow boundaries of the action itself. By nature, children want to please their parents. When a parent makes a conscious effort to overcome his inner reticence and allows his child to bring him a cup of tea, for example, the child's action causes the parent to feel gratitude toward the child. The parent then extends a kind face to the child, providing immediate positive feedback to the child's welcome behavior. A continuum of daily gestures such as these creates mutuality between parent and child. The genuine satisfaction in the parent's heart toward the child engenders satisfaction in the child's heart as well: "As water reflects a face back to a face, so one's heart is reflected back to him by another" (*Mishlei* 27:19). These seemingly simple actions create a powerful bond between parent and child, and reinforce the warm ties within the family.

Every family's daily schedule contains many opportunities for affording our children the privilege of *kibud horim* by allowing them to help us with simple actions relating to the mitzvah of "*ma'achil u'mashkeh*." Wise families take advantage of these opportunities.

Positive actions must be reinforced if we want them to repeat themselves. So when a child does something for us, it is important tell him how pleased we are. Sometimes a smile or a hug adds a great deal, or even a short thank-you note under his pillow. Of course, even when our children's "offerings" fall below the mark, we would be smart to avoid calling attention to the shortcomings.

The merit of *kibud horim* is so great that we should do our utmost to enable each one of our children as much as possible to be involved in this important mitzvah!

Tasty Morsels

Share your feelings with your children by saying such things as, "I like it when you bring me a glass of cold water on a hot day," or "I enjoyed hearing you recite Mishnayos to Zaidy on the phone." This way they learn what pleases you so that they can be considerate of your desires and needs.

When your eighteen-month-old daughter offers you an orange section she holds in her hand, don't turn her down. Even at this age, this is an opportunity teach her the mitzvah of *ma'achil u'mashkeh*.

When your son is home from yeshiva, remember to also give him the opportunity to fulfill the mitzvah of *kibud horim*.

Tell your children how pleasant it is for you to hear that they are happy and satisfied.

Your toddler can help you hang up clean laundry by offering you clothespins and articles from the laundry basket. He will also happily help you organize the vegetables and other foodstuffs from the supermarket.

Try to involve your parents in happy, gratifying "family moments," such as by calling

them up in front of your children to tell them good news. When your children see this, they will learn to involve you in the positive moments in their own lives.

Occasionally let your children prepare supper on their own, for themselves and for you as well.

Two-year-old children love to bring you your slippers. Teach them to continue to do so with the same enthusiasm even when they mature.

Children do tend to involve their parents when they have a problem. Teach them to update you when they find a solution to the problem as well.

You might find it a little embarrassing when your daughter rushes to place your coat over your shoulders when you mention that you are chilly. But if you allow her to do so, you are giving her a taste of *kibud horim* from yesteryear.

Let your children know what kinds of things you enjoy receiving from them: a flower, a note, or a picture. Encourage their giving with words of praise.

Try to say sentences such as, "Now I need...," or "I would really like it if ..." This communicates your needs and desires, and arouses your children to lending a hand.

Accustom your children to wait for Abba and Ima to enter a room first.

When Bubby comes to visit, serve as a model for your children through your good example of *kibud horim* to your mother.

Let us educate our children to give by providing encouragement and support for even their minor acts of *chessed*, such as helping Ima remove her boots and bringing Abba his winter scarf.

How lovely it is when a group of grandchildren get together to help Bubby prepare for Yom Tov or Shabbos. Bubby graciously allows her grandchildren to help her, and her good will engenders their good will.

8

Seeing the Half-Full Glass

EVERY HUMAN BEING HAS virtues and successes, as well as shortcomings and failures. Our virtues and successes represent our "half-full glass" or creative, productive abilities while our shortcomings and unfulfilled objectives are our "half-empty glass."

We usually focus on what we lack instead of what we have. There are logical grounds for our attention to the half-empty glass: as *shomrei mitzvos* who follow the traditions of our ancestors, it is clear to us that we came into this world in order to improve and perfect ourselves. Thus our life-long mission is to progress and advance in *avodas Hashem*, which causes us to focus on what we have not yet achieved and not to rest on the laurels of previous accomplishments. Our gaze is always forward into unconquered territory as we forge ahead to change what still needs to be changed.

The problem is that we tend to apply the same measures to our children as we apply to ourselves. Since we improve ourselves by concentrating on our deficiencies, we also focus on the deficiencies of our children while paying a lot less attention to their positive attributes. This is our mistake. When raising children, we must emphasize the positive elements of their behavior in order to give them the incentive, encouragement, and drive to continue in a positive direction.

The individual, whose actions in the present are rooted in the memory of positive accomplishments in the past, believes in his ability to keep working on himself in order to reach spiritual goals with Hashem's help. In contrast, dwelling on deficiencies does not inspire a person to work and make an effort. Just as we cannot build a proper building on weak structural foundations, so we cannot accomplish our personal objectives while focusing on our personal defects and shortcomings. Instead, we can only create new accomplishments on the firm foundation of old accomplishments. Wallowing in our own negativism only weakens us and undermines our strength to succeed, while identification with our positive side is what gives us the energy to persevere.

We mothers must realize that it takes practice in order to see the half-full glass. One way to begin the process is to examine ourselves and the daily work that HaKadosh Baruch Hu has assigned to us, giving us the privilege of being His partners in raising our children. How much strength has He bestowed on us to carry out our myriad activities for the family and the home! Have we ever taken a time-out from our daily "treadmill" to examine our achievements as mothers in one single morning of an average day? If we collect all the *Modeh Ani*'s that are said by our children under our guidance, all the *netilas yadayim*'s carried out under our careful instruction, we will start to feel the blessings of Hashem that, in our merit, fill our home from the earliest hours of the day. Think of the importance of such an ostensibly simple task as preparing sandwiches for children to take to school and cheder. Those sandwiches give our children the strength to study diligently and the opportunity to make the blessings of *ha-motzi* and *birkas ha-mazon*! How wonderful to think that our children will also bless us, their parents, in *birkas ha-mazon* when they say, "*Harachaman*, May the Compassionate One bless my father, my teacher and my mother, my teacher"—all the result of our sandwich-making!

We often bless others and ourselves that we may have the *zechus* to raise our children "*l'Torah, l'chuppah, u'lma'asim tovim*" and here, during two hours of a run-of-the-mill morning, we have helped actualize these Godly objectives through the simple, everyday activity of making lunch for our children. Let us appreciate our manifold accomplishments more frequently, because it is this kind of outlook and approach that imbues us with renewed strength every morning of every single day.

Appreciating the half-full glass floods our lives with great light; we need merely to infuse it into the "dark corners." An outlook such as this enables us to recognize what we have as well as what we have accomplished, and to thank the Creator of the universe for all He has given us.

Many of us fail to appreciate ourselves and the abilities we receive from Hashem due to an erroneous belief that recognition of our virtues is arrogance. But this is not the case. Arrogance is when we ascribe our powers to ourselves and only ourselves. But when we recognize that all of our character traits, talents and capabilities were not created by ourselves but rather were *bestowed* on us through Hashem's kindness, then recognition of our strengths is not arrogance but a tribute to Hashem—which only increases the honor of Heaven. In fact, it is an obligation to be grateful to the Giver, to appreciate the good from the Source of good. Instead of being mired in our own sense of power and self-importance, we become strengthened and uplifted.

The Creator of the universe equipped us with the materials with which to build our lives. How can we build without acknowledging the wonderful equipment given to us? Those who do not discover their virtues and accomplishments are likely to come to the conclusion that they lack the means with which to succeed, which thus makes it impossible for them to demand effort of themselves and to be blamed for their lack of achievement. Refusal to recognize personal strengths turns into an excuse for doing nothing, and often leads to a strong sense of deprivation and unfairness for not receiving the gifts that others seem to have been blessed with.

In contrast, how great are the capabilities of a person who invests time and effort in uncovering the "tools" Hashem has blessed him with, and who knows that he is obligated to use them for the good. The more he uncovers his strengths, the more effort he will put into rectifying himself and his world via his gifts. Rabbi Yisrael Salanter once said, "It is sad if a person does not know his weaknesses, but far more tragic is the failure to recognize his strengths, for those strengths are the primary tools of his Divine service."

A positive outlook toward ourselves engenders hope and distances us from apathy and despair. Uncovering the half-full glass raises our self-esteem and transforms our confidence to renewed activity and effort.

Parents who see their children's good qualities, emphasize the positive, and preserve their children's success experiences for them, enable their children to achieve their creative potential. A child who discovers that she is capable wants to go to the next accomplishment. She believes she can advance further because she has experienced progress before, and knows how to tackle additional challenges. With *siyatta diShmaya*, she will go forward toward future successes.

Practice finding the positive in every situation—staying home on a rainy day, for example, even though a picnic was planned—and express your positive thoughts out loud by statements such as, "Who would ever have imagined that it would be so much fun to eat our picnic sandwiches on the living room floor!"

Stop by the bed of each sleeping child to thank Hashem for gracing you with each son and daughter.

Keep a written list in a notebook about daily *nachas* you get from your children. Occasionally read the list out loud to your family so that everyone can enjoy it. You can even turn it into a quiz: "Which of the children visited Zelda, the elderly widow next door, after she came home from the hospital?" Whoever guesses can get a small prize.

Surprise your children with photos you took of them when they weren't looking—when they were helping each other perhaps, or when they were happily engaged in a family project together. Then hang the picture on the wall. You can also prepare a tape of a "happy hour" when the children were playing together.

Here's a foolproof "recipe" for a positive outlook on life: Always try to express positive feelings in words: "I enjoyed ...," "Now I am relaxed and calm," "I hope that...," "How fortunate that..."

Instead of dwelling on yesterday's mistakes, spend your time on tomorrow's hopes.

In moments of disappointment, let us hearten ourselves and those around us by saying, "*Gam zu l'tovah*, this too is for the best."

When faced with a very large load to carry, it is best to break it up into smaller, more manageable packages. The same is true for worries: when we dismantle one large worry—such as making Pesach when a child is in the hospital—into many "smaller worries," it will be easier to deal with and find solutions.

Let us ask our children, "What can we surprise Abba with today when he comes home from work?" or "Who knows what will make Naftali happy on his birthday?"

Watch how your baby claps her hands when she is pleased with herself. Don't we owe ourselves that kind of congratulations and encouragement sometimes?

Pay special attention to statements you overhear in the

house that express family togetherness and unity. Write them down (together with the names of the family members who uttered the words) and hang the page on the wall.

Sometimes, we need to use a magnifying glass to see the spot of light in a dark corner of our family life.

Let us emphasize how special Shabbos is to us by saying things such as, “On Shabbos, everyone is together at home,” or “On Shabbos, Ima has time to tell stories and listen to everyone.”

Let us emphasize family togetherness by such expressions as, “This is what we discuss around the Shabbos table in our family,” or “That’s what our family likes to do on vacation,” or “We have a secret password in our family.” These kinds of expressions facilitate a cohesive, united family unit.

Let us direct out children’s attention to *Niflaos HaBoreh*, Hashem’s miracles. For example, remind them to look at the beauty of the tree outside the window, especially when its leaves turn brown in the fall and bloom again in the spring. Has a bird made its nest in the tree? Try to gather the children together periodically to keep track of the nest—the hatching and growth of the young chicks, one stage after another.

Instead of being ensnared in the negative, it's best to focus on the positive.

Instead of comparing your achievements with someone else's, it's better to compare your own achievements of today with those of yesterday.

During moments of happiness and satisfaction, why not drop everything to enjoy the moment; let yourself bask in your *nachas* and breathe it into your very soul. Then, during difficult family moments, you can retrieve your lovely "*nachas* memories" and allow them to strengthen you.

Sit with your children and observe everything in the room. Let each one take turns saying, "How good it is that we have...," and explaining why.

Let each of the children describe three objects he or she owns, and why he or she enjoys them so much.

A wonderful way to learn innocent and pure joy is by watching our infant.

Let each child pick one of the limbs of the body and express his or her thanks to Hashem Yisbarach for the use of that limb. For example, "I thank Hashem for my two ears to hear my Ima's stories on Friday nights," or "I thank Hashem for my two legs that allow me to play soccer with my friends during recess."

You certainly cuddle your children and pat them affectionately numerous times a day. But do you remember to give yourself the same kind of positive feedback for all the things you do as an *Eim b'Yisrael*—a Mother in Israel?

Glossary

Abba: father, daddy.
al pi darko: "according to [a child's] nature" (see MISHLEI 131:2).
Am Yisrael: the Jewish People.
arba'ah minim: the "four species" taken on the Jewish Festival of Sukkos.
avodas Hashem: service of God.
b'ezras Hashem: with God's help.
bal tashchis: the prohibition against wasting.
baruch Hashem: "Thank God!"
berachos: blessings.
birkas ha-mazon: grace after meals.
bitachon: trust in God.
Bubby: (Yid.) grandma.
Chazal: an acronym for "Our Sages of blessed memory."
cheder: (Yid.) a Jewish primary school for boys.
chessed: loving-kindness.
chinuch [*banim*]: childrearing, education.
Chol HaMoed: the intermediate days of the Jewish Festivals of Passover and Sukkos.
Chumash: the Five Books of Moses.
da'as Torah: the TORAH-based opinions of recognized rabbinic authorities.
da'as: an opinion or idea.
daven: (Yid.) pray.
Devarim: the book of Deuteronomy.
emunah: faith in God.
erev Shabbos: the day before the Sabbath, i.e. Friday.
gedolei Torah: TORAH leaders.
gemach: a free-loan society.
HaKadosh Baruch Hu: the Holy One, blessed is He (i.e., God).
ha-motzi: the blessing recited before eating bread.
Hashem: God.
hashgachah: Divine providence.
im yirtzeh Hashem: God-willing.
Ima: mother, mommy.
kaf zechus/lechaf zechus: the benefit of the doubt.
kallah: a bride.
kavanah: concentration, intention.
kedushah: holiness.
kibud horim: the MITZVAH of honoring parents.
lichvod Shabbos [*kodesh*]: "in honor of [the holy] Sabbath."
mikarev levavos: forging a connection between two people.
Mishlei: the book of Proverbs.
mishnayos: paragraphs of Mishnah.

mitzvah/*mitzvos*: commandment(s), good deed(s).
mitzvas aseh: a positive commandment.
mitzvas lo sa'aseh: a negative commandment.
morei hora'ah: decisors of Jewish law.
mussar: TORAH ethics and values aimed at character improvement.
nachas: pleasure.
neshamah yeseirah: the "extra soul" we possess on the Sabbath.
netilas yadayim: the ritual washing of the hands.
oneg Shabbos: enjoyment of the Sabbath.
pesukim: Biblical verses.
peyos: sidelocks.
rebbe: a TORAH teacher.
refuah: recovery.
Ribbono shel Olam: Master of the universe (i.e., God).
sefarim, *sifrei kodesh*: holy books.
Shabbos: the Sabbath.
she'eilah: a question on Jewish law.
Shem Shamayim: the Name of Heaven.
Shemos: the book of Exodus.
shep nachas: (Yid.) to reap pleasure.
shev v'al ta'aseh: keeping the status quo in times of doubt.
Sheva Berachos: the festive meals held the first seven days after a Jewsh wedding.
shomrei mitzvos: those who observe the MITZVOS.
shuk: a marketplace.
simchah: joy.
siyatta diShmaya: help from Heaven.
Tanach: an acronym for the Old Testament.
tefillah: prayer.
Tehillim: the book of Psalms.
tinokos she-nishbu: Jews not raised with religious upbringing.
Torah: the Five Books of Moses; the whole corpus of Jewish tradition.
Toras imecha: "The TORAH imbibed from your mother."
tzaddik(im): righteous individual(s).
tzedakah: charity.
Vayikra: the book of Leviticus.
yasher koach: "Good for you!"
yeshiva: an academy of TORAH study.
yeshuah: salvation.
yetzer ha-ra: the evil inclination.
yiras Shamayim: fear of Heaven.
Yom Tov: a Jewish holiday.
Zaidy: (Yid.) grandpa.
zechus: merit.